God's Presence
Makes the World

God's Presence Makes the World

The Celtic Vision through the Centuries in Wales

A.M. ALLCHIN

DARTON·LONGMAN + TODD

First published 1997 by
Darton, Longman and Todd Ltd
1 Spencer Court
140–142 Wandsworth High Street
London SW18 4JJ

ISBN 0–232–52206–5

A catalogue record for this book is available
from the British Library.

Thanks are due to the following for permission to reproduce copyright
material:
Borddas (Gwasg Dinefwr) for extracts from *Bobi Jones: Selected Poems* (1987)
by Joseph P. Clancy, and *Blodeugerdd Barddas O Ganu Crefyddol Cynnar* (1994)
by Marged Haycock;
Church in Wales Publications for extracts from *Euros Bowen, Priest-Poet*
(1995) edited by C. and S. Davies;
Gomer Press for extracts from *Iolo Goch: Poems* (1993) by Dafydd Johnston,
and a poem by Gwenallt in *Poetry of Wales 1930–70* (1974) by R Gerallt
Jones;
Modern Poetry in Translation No. 7 (1995), Welsh issue, for extracts from
poems by Gwyneth Lewis;
Oxford University Press for extracts from *Jeremy Taylor, Holy Living* (1989)
edited by P. G. Stanwood;
Papermac (Macmillan Publishers) for the extract from *The Echoes Return Slow*
(1988) by R. S. Thomas;
Seren (Poetry Wales Press) for extracts from *Welsh Airs* (1987) by R. S.
Thomas, and *Welsh Verse* (1986) by Tony Conran;
SPCK for the translation of a poem by Dafydd ap Gwilym in *Celtic Christian
Spirituality* (1995) edited by Oliver Davies and Fiona Bowie;
University of Wales Press for extracts from *Celtic Christianity in Early
Medieval Wales* (1996) by Oliver Davies, and Saunders Lewis, *Selected Poems*
(1993) translated by Joseph P. Clancy.

Phototypeset in 11/13¾pt Adobe Caslon by Intype London Ltd
Printed and bound in Great Britain by
Page Bros, Norwich

cyflwynir y llyfr hwn

i

Idris Llewelyn Foster
(1911–1984)

a

Bedwyr Lewis Jones
(1933–1992)

Athrawon Cymraeg a
Chyfeillion Gwerthfawr Iawn.

Uwch ein clai Dy serch a'n clwm.

CONTENTS

ACKNOWLEDGEMENTS

In writing a book of this kind which surveys a large area in a comparatively brief space, the writer is aware at every point of depending on the work of scholars who have studied particular questions in detail and in depth. The references at the end of the book record something of this indebtedness. To two friends I am particularly grateful, Dr Oliver Davies of the University of Wales, Lampeter, who allowed me to make use of the text of his vitally important book *Celtic Christianity in Early Medieval Wales* when it was still in typescript, and Mr Paul Quinn of the Centre for Higher Welsh and Celtic Studies of the University of Wales, Aberystwyth, for his constant encouragement, stimulus and support.

Anyone who works in this field soon becomes aware of the debt which is owed to the two outstanding translators of Welsh poetry in our time, Tony Conran and Joseph Clancy. I am specially grateful to Tony Conran for permission to quote from his forthcoming book on Waldo Williams, again a work which I have been able to consult in typescript.

I hope that this book will be read in conjunction with my earlier study, *Praise Above All; Discovering the Welsh Tradition* (University of Wales Press, 1991). It will be evident that both books have it as their primary aim to reveal the truth and beauty, the inward unity and coherence of the Christian faith as it is presented in this tradition. But both books also have a more local and limited objective, and that is to point to the conviction expressed in the earlier work that 'it is Wales which holds the key to the preservation of the personality of Britain, *yr ynys hon*, whose true unity is precisely *not* a uniformity'.

PREFACE

The major part of this book is based on six lectures given in Bangor in the first months of 1996. The lectures were given under the auspices of the Cathedral and formed part of the celebration of the 1450th anniversary of the diocese. I am most grateful to the Dean, The Very Reverend Erwyd Edwards, for the invitation to give the lectures and thus to contribute to the diocesan celebration of its first bishop, St Deiniol. Preparing the material for the lectures gave me the occasion to work out more clearly thoughts about the Christian tradition in Wales and its relation to Celtic Christianity as a whole. These thoughts have been stimulated in recent years not least by a growing awareness of the remarkable international interest in this subject of Celtic Christianity.

The first six chapters of the book succeed one another in chronological order. But whereas the earliest period is treated in some detail in the first two chapters, and chapters five and six are devoted to the poets of our own century, the two intervening chapters have to cover the seven hundred years from 1200–1900 and are necessarily very selective. The final chapter draws together some of the themes treated in the main part of the book.

In all I hope that certain common themes and major lines

of direction emerge. One cannot go very far into the Welsh heritage without discovering that one is dealing with a tradition which has an astonishing sense of inner continuity through the centuries. A Methodist poet of the late eighteenth century may write in the style and spirit of the middle ages; the particular view of Christology which we find in poets in the tenth century is found again in the poets of our own time.

The material presented here is therefore intended to be at least implicitly, and sometimes indeed explicitly, a response to the kind of questions which are often asked about Celtic Christianity. What exactly is it? Is it something solely of the past or does it still exist today? Is it a form of Christianity altogether unique and different from others? Is it something based in the realities of flesh and blood, or is it largely a matter of fantasy, a creation of our own imagination?

The answers given in the pages which follow are based on the study of actual places and people, of people of past centuries and our own, of what they have said and done, and of what they are still saying and doing. The centre of our attention is Wales, but insofar as we are trying to discern common elements of Celtic faith and understanding, the other Celtic countries, Ireland and Scotland, Cornwall and Brittany, are not altogether forgotten.

What then is the general impression of Celtic Christianity which emerges from this enquiry? As we see it in its early classical period, before about 1200, it is a Christian tradition which in its basic structures of faith and understanding is trinitarian and incarnational, and thus profoundly orthodox, firmly rooted in the common Christendom of East and West in the first millennium of our era. But it is a tradition which holds together the doctrine of creation and the doctrine of redemption with particular clarity and vigour. The relationship of these two doctrines to one another is grounded in a vision of Christ the Word as at once creator of all things as well as their redeemer.

This vision is of course firmly anchored in the New Testament, for instance in the fourth gospel or in the Pauline epistles, especially Ephesians and Colossians with their understanding of the reconciliation of all things in God through the cross of Christ (Colossians 1:15–20). It is developed in the writings of the fathers particularly in their understanding of the central place of Christ in the cosmos as a whole. But in Celtic Christianity this vision receives a particular emphasis and particular development. The pattern which we know as the pattern of redemption, the pattern of incarnation, death and resurrection, is seen as vividly present in all creation, built into the structure of the universe. God's presence makes the world. This vision of the active presence of God the Word, alike in creation and redemption, is not infrequently related to the eucharist. In such a context it seems appropriate, to use the phrase of Teilhard de Chardin, to speak of 'the Mass on the World'.

In Wales, as we shall see, this vision is carried forward and expressed through a particular understanding and practice of the art of poetry, seen as a sacred art to be offered in God's service and exercised in God's praise. The poet fulfils a representative, indeed a priestly, role, speaking on behalf of his fellow human beings and on behalf of all creation. As Dylan Thomas said, 'These poems were written for the love of Man and in praise of God, and I'd be a damn fool if they weren't'.

In the early Celtic world the exercise of artistic skill was not of course confined to the art of poetry. One of the remarkable characteristics of the Christianity of this period is its ability to inspire great works of sacred art, in stone carving, in metal work, in manuscript illumination. Here the contribution of Ireland is particularly rich. In all this field Celtic Christianity surely owes much to the pre-Christian civilisation of the Celts, a civilisation which lies behind the development of the early Christian centuries and is often incorporated into it. Eloquent speech and song seem to have been characteristic of the Celtic peoples as long as we have any record of them.

In one sense the story which the pages of this book seek to unfold is the story of a tradition which has lived in a certain isolation from the outside world and has jealously guarded its own inner coherence and integrity. But it is a tradition which has never altogether ceased to assimilate material from outside, whether it is Dafydd ap Gwilym meditating on the *Anima Christi*, Ellis Wynne translating Jeremy Taylor, or Euros Bowen pondering the frescoes and icons of Constantinople and Crete. Its continuing interaction with the life of the Christian world as a whole is stronger than might at first appear; its significance for the recovery of Christian unity, as will be suggested in the last chapter, greater than has usually been recognised.

Living in a city like Bangor, where the two old-established linguistic and cultural traditions of southern Britain are both active and flourishing, demands an awareness of the presence of both and of the possibility of interchange between them. It is at once a privilege and a challenge to live in such a place. The Cathedral on the one side, the lineal descendant of the community founded by St Deiniol in the sixth century, the University on the other, now more than a century old, speak of these possibilities of collaboration and interchange. The presence of the University, which, in particular through its Welsh department, has contributed greatly to the study of the language, literature and history of Wales in the last hundred years, is at once a resource and an encouragement.

The paradox, indeed in some moods one is inclined to say the tragedy of the present situation, not only in Bangor but throughout Great Britain, is that for the vast majority of people, even of those who concern themselves with the things of the mind and the spirit, the older of these traditions might as well not exist. It remains an almost wholly unknown land. I hope these pages may convey something of the excitement I have felt in recent years in penetrating further into that *terra incognita*.

I speak of a sense of excitement advisedly for we are living at a rather extraordinary moment. The subject seems, as it were, to be coming to life under our hands. On the one side there is intense international interest and expectation; there are insistent audiences, to be found in Sussex and Cumbria and Dublin, in Texas and Massachusetts. On the other side there are new developments in the study of the subject which are making original texts and resources available for the first time.

The first two chapters of this book could not have been written had it not been for two recent acquisitions; the English translations made by Dr Oliver Davies with a view to his own work *Celtic Christianity in Early Medieval Wales: The Origins of the Welsh Spiritual Tradition* (1996) and the invaluable edition of the early poems, *Blodeugerdd Barddas O Ganu Crefyddol Cynnar* made by Dr Marged Haycock and published in 1994. That volume gives the reader the text of some thirty-three poems together with a literal translation into modern Welsh and invaluable notes and commentary. All this has become available in the last three years.

The sources are not always so easily available. Often the original texts are very difficult to come by. From the later middle ages, as we suggest in chapter three, there are, for instance, vital poetic texts as yet unpublished. With regard to other writers whose work is more accessible, it is often the case that the religious meaning of their work has been very little discussed. From the time of early Methodism, the prose of Thomas Jones of Denbigh, surely a remarkable resource for

Christian spirituality, remains altogether unexplored. Of the theological poetry of our own century it is true that we now have more translations into English, particularly in the case of Bobi Jones and Euros Bowen. But again there is much that waits to be done. There are of course writers of the greatest importance whose work is not even mentioned here, pre-eminent among them Morgan Llwyd, a contemporary, and in some ways counterpart of George Fox.

Nonetheless, a process of rediscovery seems to have begun, and if we turn from texts to places we find something similar is happening. Ancient and forgotten shrines have been coming to new life in the last decade. Ynys Enlli/Bardsey Island is once again a place of pilgrimage and retreat. At Pennant Melangell, in the Berwyns, the restoration of the saint's shrine in 1992 has been followed by a renewal of the place itself as a centre of prayer and healing. In South Wales the ancient Marian shrine of Penrhys has come to life again in a remarkable ecumenical venture linked directly with the creation of new forms of community life and service in a notably deprived urban area.

All these are things which are happening now and which carry promise for the future. Thus, a book which at first sight might appear to be altogether about the past, opens out on to new perspectives. Certainly there is a wealth of material left to us by our predecessors in the faith, which deserves to be explored, material which can strengthen and encourage us in the present. But this heritage is not only a thing of the past. It is alive now and so looking to the future, looking for a genuine rediscovery of the tradition of Celtic Christianity not only in the Celtic countries but more universally, and in Britain looking specifically to a new, more just and fruitful relationship between the two languages Welsh and English. Let the last word of this preface come from the latest poet which it celebrates.

Cherish the dark's obscurity
Look for the diamonds in debris,
Thank God for all His mystery
and LIVE.

CHAPTER ONE

Letters Cannot Contain It:

The Earliest Witnesses

In this book I mean to look at Celtic spirituality primarily in its Welsh manifestation. We shall turn to other parts of the Celtic world simply for parallels, comparisons and contrasts. In the first two chapters I intend to concentrate on the earliest religious poetry; in the last two we shall consider the poetry of our own century. The intervening period, almost a thousand years, will necessarily be treated in a very selective way in chapters three and four.

The growth and development of Christianity in the early centuries of our era, in the western part of the island of Britain which we now call Wales began and was carried forward in a situation of extreme difficulty. The collapse of the Roman Empire and the withdrawal of Roman troops in AD 410 was followed by a period of widespread confusion which was compounded by the invasion of the island by Germanic tribes from the continent of Europe. The amazing thing is that from this situation a church and a people emerged, which if their outward history has often been troubled and constricted, has inwardly discovered extraordinary riches. A Welsh poet of our own time, Waldo Williams, replies to the question 'What is Life?', with the words 'Finding a large room between narrow walls'. It might serve as a motto for this people through the ages.

When we come to examine the origins of the Christian tradition in Wales we are struck at once by a foundational fact which clearly distinguishes the Welsh from the English situation. In Wales there is an unbroken history going back into the period of the Roman Empire, into the Christian communities of Roman Britain. It is almost certainly the case that Christianity was not strongly represented in the first four centuries of our era in much of the geographical area now called Wales. But in the south-east, on the border with Herefordshire, and along parts of the south coast, the Christianity of Roman Britain was strongly present. The names of the martyrs Julius and Aaron at Caerleon remind us of this fact. Coming into the century after the departure of the Roman army, the figure of Dyfrig as a diocesan bishop and of Illtyd as the abbot of a monastery with a high reputation as a centre of learning, speak of a continuity of life which points us back into the period before AD 410.

Something of the flavour of that post-Roman Britain is conveyed by an inscription found near Cynwyl Gaeo and now conserved in the museum at Carmarthen. It is one of the two Latin inscriptions in Wales to be written in verse and it is reckoned to date from about AD 520:

> *Servator Fidei, Patriaeque Semper Amator*
> *Hic Paulinus Iacit Cultor Pientissimus Aequi.*

'A guardian of the faith, of his homeland always a lover, here Paulinus lies; most conscientious observer of all that is right.'[1] Caeo was an important centre of the Roman occupation of this area, the place where the gold mining operations were centred. It is not therefore surprising to find a cultivated Latin inscription here; but even so someone in that early sixth century must have been intensely conservative. The inscription, with its phrases borrowed from classical Latin verse, breathes a sense of security and assurance which can hardly have been typical of Dyfed at that time. Yet still it is there; Romanitas had not entirely disappeared.

We only have to contrast these two lines with those of the only other Latin verse inscription from the early Christian centuries of Wales to feel all the difference between the sixth and the seventh century, between Carmarthen and the country round Builth:

> *In Sindone Muti, Ioruert Ruallaunque Sepultus*
> *Iudicii Adventum, Spectant In Pace Tremendum.*

'Silent in the shroud, Iorwerth and Ruallan await in peace the dreadful coming of the Judgement.'[2] This inscription is to be found in the little church of Llanlleonfel, a place otherwise renowned for the wedding of Charles Wesley to Sarah Gwynne in 1749. The Welsh tradition, it tells us, has its origins in a situation where civil order has collapsed and where all earthly securities are taken away. The conversion of the peoples of this land to Christianity took place in the midst of the death and destruction of an old order. Men and women were faced with a naked encounter with ultimate realities, with death and judgement. However affirmative the Christianity of these centuries may be, it is never altogether comfortable or assured about life in this world; the reality of another world is too close.

Some people would feel that this other-worldly pressure has remained a feature of Welsh Christianity down till today. Here we have no abiding city but we seek one to come. But because the cross is carved in the middle of this seventh-century inscription, the death of the old order can be taken into Christ's death and so the two warriors near Builth can rest in peace. On death and judgement follows resurrection.

For if the situation of the Cymry, as the British people of

the west came to call themselves, was in some sense constricted, the life which they lived was full of an awareness of space and possibility, a space and possibility given by the faith which they had embraced so wholeheartedly. To the old pre-Christian sense of an iron fate which determines all things, an awareness of the world as wholly hemmed in by death, there succeeded a vision of human life in all its fragility as open to the eternity of God. This is not only an openness to an eternity beyond this world, it is an openness to an eternal life already made known and experienced now.

One of the most striking things which marks these early Christian centuries in Wales is the sense that God's grace is present and at work now, evident in the diversity and richness of creation, and in the way in which apparent opposites belong together and are at one. This is true not only of creation as a whole but also, specifically, in the life of the Christian community, the church.

Consider for an instant two other early Latin inscriptions, both from the sixth century, to be found in North Wales. First there is a well-known memorial from near Aberdaron which commemorates Senacus the presbyter, *Cum Multitudinem Fratrum*.[3] This carefully inscribed stone which also dates from about AD 520 has always been understood as a monument commemorating an early monastic community, the beginnings indeed of the community of Enlli (Bardsey Island). It is a witness to the importance of monasticism at the origins of Christianity in Wales.

Then turn to a monument found in Anglesey, dating from the same period. 'Here lies a most holy woman, the very loving wife of Bivatigornis, servant of God, bishop and disciple of Paulinus . . .'[4] This was a church which honoured monastic life highly and placed the monastic communities at the heart of its life. At the same time this was a church which had a highly honoured married clergy. It was to stay that way for a thousand years. For instance, in the eleventh century Sulien, Bishop of St David's, was father of three outstanding clerics and scholars. The celibate discipline of the Latin church was never altogether accepted in Wales. Indeed, on the question of the relationship of the monastery to the Christian community as a whole, despite differences between Wales and Ireland, it is clear that throughout the Celtic world, in the early centuries, the contrasting and complementary vocations were held together in close unity.[5]

I

If the inscriptions on the monuments give us some small glimpse into the life of these early centuries we have to recognise that it is not till later that we begin to have direct evidence in writing for the faith and devotion of this early Celtic world in Britain. As we come through the centuries we meet with one text which we can date quite closely, the verses in the *Juvencus* manuscript which comes from the ninth century.

The manuscript is now in the university library in Cambridge. It contains Juvencus' fourth-century Latin metrical version of the gospels and in the margins a number of glosses and notes, some in Latin, some in Welsh, some in Irish. It is generally agreed that these additions were made in the first half of the tenth century. Thus the poem we are about to consider, which is placed in a prominent position in the margin at the top of the first page, is certainly the oldest text of a theological poem existing in Welsh.

The manuscript, it seems clear, was written in the scriptorium of a monastery in Wales, in a community in which Welsh and Irish monks were living side by side. It is reasonable to suppose that such a community may have been in west Wales, where Irish contacts were frequent and close; perhaps in St David's in the south, possibly at Llanbadarn Fawr in mid Wales, possibly in Bangor in the north. Whatever precise geographical location we give to the writing of this poem we can be confident that it comes from a monastic milieu in which the inherited wisdom of the two main branches of the early Celtic Christian world, the Goidelic and Brythonic, was cultivated and studied.

The text of the poem in the manuscript has been damaged. The translation which follows makes it clear that the first verse of the poem is incomplete. The same thing is in part true of verse six. What we have here is a reconstruction of that verse on the part of the translator, a responsible but necessarily hypothetical reconstruction:

Almighty Creator, it is you who have made
the land and the sea . . .

The world cannot comprehend in song bright and
    melodious,
even though the grass and trees should sing,
all your wonders, O true Lord!

The Father created the world by a miracle;
It is difficult to express its measure.
Letters cannot contain it, letters cannot comprehend it.

Jesus created for the hosts of Christendom,
with miracles when he came,
resurrection through his nature.

He who made the wonder of the world,
will save us, has saved us.
It is not too great toil to praise the Trinity.

Clear and high in the perfect assembly,
let us praise above the nine grades of angels
the sublime and blessed Trinity.

Purely, humbly, in skilful verse,
I should love to give praise to the Trinity,
according to the greatness of his power.

God has required of the host in this world
who are his, that they should at all times,
all together, fear the Trinity.

The one who has power, wisdom and dominion
above heaven, below heaven, completely;
it is not too great toil to praise the Son of Mary.[6]

In terms of its language and style the poem can be compared with a large group of secular poems, which date from this same period, the poems of the Llywarch Hen and Heledd sagas. These poems connect the earliest period of Welsh poetry, dating from the sixth century, with the much more abundant material produced from the twelfth century onward by the poets of the Princes.

Dr Jenny Rowland of the University of Dublin, in her masterly study of this material, *Early Welsh Saga Poetry*, says of this particular poem, 'despite some gaps in the text and linguistic difficulties, it is clear that this is praise poetry to the Trinity of a high order. The chief glory of the poem is its metrical structure with verbal repetition formed in overlapping and cyclical patterns, as in some of the most sophisticated poems in *Canu Heledd*.' She notes, moreover, in stanzas three to five, 'the unique use, in the early Englynion, of three consecutive synonyms as the *gair cyrch*', that is to say the last word in the first line in each stanza, which in the

7

original metrical scheme is a word which receives special emphasis.

It is Dr Rowland's judgement that the 'subject matter and expression of the poem are fairly stereotyped'.[7] I shall suggest, however, that this is not the case and that the content of the poem is every bit as sophisticated and carefully thought through as the form. As is often the case in classical Welsh verse, form and content are very closely related.

The work is a poem in praise of God as Trinity, as creator, redeemer, sanctifier. Very suitably it consists of nine verses. However, they are not arranged as we might expect in three groups of three. Rather it seems that verses one, two and nine belong together, while verses three to five and six to eight form two successive Trinitarian sequences. We are of course hampered in our approach to the poem by the fact that a large part of the first verse has not survived. We shall come back to this point later, noting only that the Latin words *Omnipotens Auctor* are retained in the original. This use of Latin suggests a quasi-liturgical character for the text.

Verses two and three both express the conviction, very typical of the poetry of this period, that the glory of God goes altogether beyond creation's power to express it. Even if every leaf on every tree and every blade of grass should sing, as in fact the poet implies they do, they would never reach the sum of praise. Our words, whether spoken or written, can never contain, never totally comprehend the realities of which they speak. This is true for the things of this world and still more true for the mysteries of God. This does not mean that words only point to things, as it were, from outside. They really make present, in a mysterious way, the things they refer to.

The early Celtic Christians were in no doubt about the power of words. A blessing could give life and a curse could kill. One of the most disconcerting characteristics of some of the early Welsh saints is the frequency with which they use

8

this power of cursing. But words, though powerful to create and to destroy, never totally contain the reality that they refer to. Thus the saint is not in the end a magician. The power he exercises is not his own but God's.

Words do not give us total control over the things they name. There is always something more. They need always to be seen in relationship with one another, to be understood in the context of other words. Still more they need to be seen in relationship to the people who use them. Their purpose is to establish communication, communion between people and between the world and God. The Romanian word for 'word' is helpful to us here, it is *cuvint*, from the Latin *Conventum*; a word is a meeting place.

The first strictly Trinitarian group of verses in the poem begins with the Father in verse three (here again the Latin word *Pater* occurs in the Welsh). It goes on in the next verse to speak of Jesus and in the third it comes anonymously to 'the one who made the wonder of the world'. We need not hesitate to see in this verse a reference to the third person of the Trinity, at work both in creation and in redemption, at work indeed in our own present activity, enabling and inspiring the praise of God the Trinity in which the poet is engaged, and which begins explicitly in the last line of the verse.

The second group of three verses, six to eight, act out the praise of the Trinity of which the first group has spoken. In verse six God is praised in heaven and on earth. The nine orders of angels are specifically mentioned. In verse eight the whole of God's people on earth are charged with this duty. In between, in verse seven, the poet speaks out clearly in his own name with a blending of humility before God and a pride in his skill as a writer. This blend of humility and pride is, as we shall see, very characteristic of the Welsh religious poetry of this period; poetic art is seen as a divine gift but it demands to

9

be cultivated. In these three verses we find a conjunction of cosmic, corporate and personal acts of praise, again very typical of the religious verse of this time.

We turn now to look at the two verses with which the poem begins and the verse with which it ends. Granted the incomplete nature of verse one, it may be wise to start with verse nine. Very often in Celtic poetry the purpose of the whole is found at the end and very often the end involves the recapitulation of the beginning. The last line of the poem speaks clearly of Christ in his humanity, 'it is not too great toil to praise the son of Mary'. The first line of the same verse with its evocation of the one who has power, wisdom and dominion, surely points to Christ in his divinity, with its echoes of the hymns of praise to the Lamb, to be found in the book of Revelation. Taken together it seems that this last stanza speaks of a union of the human and the divine in the person of the incarnate Lord.

What then of the beginning? It has usually been assumed that the first line is addressed to God the Father. But the title *Omnipotens Auctor* is not necessarily addressed to the first person of the Trinity alone. In fact, in Irish liturgical texts, both collects and hymns, *Omnipotens* and *Auctor* are terms at times used of the Son, by whom all things were made. In the Anglo-Saxon verses on the Ruthwell Cross (late seventh century) Christ is spoken of as Almighty God. May it not be that the poem is addressed primarily to God the Word? If this is so, then the whole act of trinitarian praise which the poem contains is set within a deliberately incarnational framework.

If this interpretation is correct, what we have here is a poem in which the praise and celebration of God as Trinity is indissolubly bound up with the praise and celebration of the mystery of the incarnation. In a way appropriate to his poetic art the poet has suggested the interrelationship of the two foundation doctrines of patristic Christianity. But to appreciate the skill of this poem we need to look more carefully at the three synonyms in verses three, four and five, which Jenny Rowland found so striking from a literary point of view, each of them words which signify 'world'. We shall find them no less interesting in terms of theology.

II

These three words for world are *presen*, *bedydd* and *elfydd*. Each one was at that time a new coinage in Welsh, based on a Latin original. Each word tells us something of vital significance about how these early poets, who were also scholars and theologians, understood the world in relation to God.

The first word, *presen*, comes from *presentia* or *presens*. The world is that which is present to us, now in this moment of time, poised between past and future, here in this particular place where we find ourselves to be. But this precariously poised point in time and space is rooted and made sure in God. Thus there is a deeper meaning in the word. The world is the place of God's presence. God's presence makes the world at every moment. Without him there is no world. This means that God as creator does not leave the world he has made to its own devices. He sustains it by his constant creative act. A moment's reflection will show that on this view of things there can be a very close relationship between the world understood as the place of God's presence and the eucharist understood as the place of his particular and continuing presence in Christ.

The word *presen* seems to me to have something of the same quality as the Romanian word for 'world', *lume*, which comes from the Latin *Lumen*, light. The one word sees God's presence making the world. The other word sees our world, with all its darkness, as yet a manifestation of the uncreated

11

yet infinitely creative light of God. Both words come from moments when the revelation recorded in St John's gospel was powerfully shaping the language and perceptions of whole peoples. As the prologue of that gospel affirms of the Word made flesh, 'In him was life and the life was the light of men and the light shines in the darkness and the darkness does not overcome it.' (John 1:4–5).

The second word, *bedydd*, has an explicit sacramental reference. Its first meaning is *baptism* and it is linked with a related word *bydysawd*, still the ordinary Welsh word for universe, deriving from the Latin word *baptizatus* which means baptised. The primary meaning of both these words is Christendom, the world in which Christ is acknowledged, that part of the human race which has received baptism, the church of Christ. But both can also have a wider and fuller meaning, for both speak of creation as well as redemption. Baptism is the sacrament, the mystery of dying and rising. In it men and women are plunged into the death and resurrection of Christ and in that action, not only is their own purpose and destiny revealed and fulfilled, but also the purpose and destiny of all creation. The movement from death to life is hidden at the very heart of things.

Christ is the Word by whom all things were made. In his death and resurrection, all things were changed because he is the one in whom all things hold together from the beginning. The early Celtic theologians saw this very directly; by the resurrection of Christ the whole destiny of the world is made manifest. 'All the world rose with him, for the essence of all the elements dwelt in the body which Jesus assumed . . . Every kind of matter, every element and every essence which is seen in the world were all combined in the body in which Christ arose, that is in the body of every human being.'[8]

This brings us to the third word, *elfydd*, which comes from

12

the Latin *elementa*. It refers to the common belief of the classical and early Christian world that the world and human beings within it are made up of a number of elements, or basic building blocks. When we remember this ancient way of viewing things we usually think of four elements, earth, air, fire and water, as the components of the world and the components of the human person. But often in the early Celtic centuries people thought of seven elements; air would be doubled, calm air on the one side, cloud and tempest on the other; water would be doubled, salt water in the sea as opposed to fresh water in the streams and rivers. The seventh element out of which the world and human beings were made was *flowers*; flowers, as it was said, for the variety and beauty of the eyes of men and women.

The woman in early Welsh legend, Blodeuwedd (flowerform), the woman made of flowers, was thus not a totally artificial construction; she was a terribly unbalanced creation, like a dish made entirely out of sugar.

Out of these varied elements in the universe and in humankind, the Spirit of God creates a living world, an organic unity. As at the beginning, so still today, the Spirit broods over the waters of chaos, making of them *elfydd*, a universe, a world. The Spirit is not only giver of life but creator of life, 'everywhere present and filling all things', creating at once the diversity and variety of the world and human life and at the same time producing its coherence and unity. As we shall see in the twentieth century, Euros Bowen considered the whole purpose of his poetry to be the discernment and praise of 'the sacramental elements of the goodness present in the world'.

Such are some of the elements of God's relationship with his creation as implied in the *Juvencus Englynion*. Each of the three words we have been considering presupposes and intimates interrelationship between God's work in creation and God's work in redemption. The one supports and complements the other.

It so happens that the early Celtic Christian world produced one great philosophical theologian, the only speculative thinker between Augustine at the end of the classical period and Anselm at the beginning of the high middle ages; that is John Scotus Eriugena (c.810–c.877), the Irishman who, in the ninth century, went across to the continent at the invitation of the Emperor Charles the Bald and taught in the schools of Paris. Note that he was a contemporary of the writer of our poem 'In Praise of the Trinity', and that that poem came from a monastery in which Welsh and Irish were living in one community.

It also so happens that we have, from this time, an unusually vivid and detailed glimpse into the relations between Ireland, North Wales and the continent. In the ninth century Gwynedd had two outstanding rulers, Merfyn Frych (d.844) and his son Rhodri Fawr (Rhodri the Great, d.877). In the latter part of his reign Rhodri became ruler of almost the whole of Wales. He was a man of European reputation, not least on account of his successful defence of his kingdom from the attacks of the Vikings. John Davies, in *The History of Wales*, remarks that he alone, of ninth-century rulers, shares with Charlemagne and King Alfred the title 'Great'.

It seems at this time to have been common for Irish scholars on the way to the continent to make a stop at the royal court of Gwynedd; one of the challenges provided for the visitors, as a kind of test of the genuineness of their learning, was a cryptogram whose solution required at least an elementary knowledge of Greek. If you passed the test your standing was much enhanced! This was the world in which Eriugena grew up, in which contacts between Ireland, Britain and the continent were taken for granted, where scholars were fluent in Latin but had only the slightest hold on Greek.

How important Eriugena's Irish origins and education were in determining the future direction of his thought is a matter on which the experts have disagreed. Did his early training have a decisive influence in shaping his future studies? Certainly his fascination with the theology of the Greek fathers, Gregory of Nyssa, Pseudo-Dionysius and Maximus the Confessor, and his great abilities as a translator were things which could only develop on the continent, in the context of the Carolingian court. There, diplomatic and commercial relations with Constantinople had created a milieu in which the systematic study of the Greek language became possible, in a way which was certainly not possible at that time in Ireland.[9]

But as we have already seen, if the scholars of the early Celtic world did not know Greek, there are signs that they knew about Greek and would have wanted to know more. There are a number of clear indications that the Celtic churches were not only aware of an indebtedness to the Latin West but also of an indebtedness to the world further east, the world of Constantinople, Jerusalem and the deserts of Egypt.

It is at least surely significant that the only Latin theologian of the Middle Ages who attempted to make a synthesis of the theological vision of the Greek and Latin worlds, was this man who in his early years was nourished, spiritually and intellectually, in the monastic schools of Ireland. The desire to go further and to explore new worlds revealed in the missionary journeys of the Irish monks, whether to Iceland in the north or to Italy in the south, is here paralleled by an intellectual daring which launches out into the deepest questions of theological reflection, and

15

which seeks to see Greek East and Latin West in a single focus.

Thus the attraction which Eriugena felt to the theology of the East was not, I would suggest, something fortuitous. It is a sign of an underlying if latent affinity between the Celtic Christian world and the world of the Greek and Syrian teachers and saints.

Eriugena, as a very daring theologian, laid himself open to accusations of heresy. He has often been accused of pantheism, of saying that God is everything and everything is God. In his Gifford Lectures, John Macquarrie argues with great care and precision that this accusation of pantheism is false. Eriugena carefully maintains the distinction between God and all that he has made. He speaks as emphatically of the divine transcendence as of the divine immanence. God who is in all things, is also beyond all things. But Eriugena speaks much of that immanence. God dwells in all creation and is not to be divorced from it. 'It is clear that for him God and the world are not two separate entities, but, however different they are, belong together in a whole.'

This means that creation and redemption are seen together. What we call the incarnation and atonement, Christ's coming in the flesh, his death and resurrection, are not accidental. They reveal to us the innermost meaning and destiny of creation from the beginning. In all things God is revealing himself. Eriugena sees both movements, creation and redemption, as fundamentally at one. So he himself writes, 'That which is properly thought of as beyond all essence is also properly known in all essence and therefore every visible and invisible creature can be called a theophany, that is an appearance of the divine.'

Every visible and invisible creature is a theophany, a manifestation of the divine. But for Eriugena a theophany is not only a manifestation of the divine; following the great Greek

16

theologian of the seventh century, Maximus the Confessor, whose work Eriugena translated into Latin, a theophany is as Macquarrie says, 'To be understood as an active self communication of God, in and through the things of the world.'[10] The principle of the incarnation works itself out in an indefinitely large number of ways, for as Maximus maintains, 'The Word of God, who is God, wills at all times and in all places to work the mystery of his embodiment'.

So an outstanding twentieth-century exponent of Maximus, the Romanian theolgian Dumitru Staniloae, would constantly say, 'The world is God's word and God's gift to us; and God is present to us in his word and in his gift.' Or as Macquarrie puts it, 'All things in the created order, from the highest to the lowest may be the occasion of a theophany.'

III

The poem in praise of the Trinity which we have been looking at is unusual for many reasons, not least because we can date it fairly exactly. There is one other smaller set of verses written in a similar style which may come from the same period, and which at any rate is likely to go back well before the year 1100. This is a poem in celebration of the incarnation, centred on the mother of the Lord. For the early centuries in the Celtic West, as in all the other parts of the old Christian world, East and West, the praise of Mary is inseparably linked with the confession of faith that Jesus is the incarnate Word:

> Mary nurtures a Son in her womb:
> His birth a blessing to those who discover him.
> He goes forth like the sun, great is the number of his
> company.

Mary nurtures a Son at her breast:
His birth a blessing to those who see him.
He goes forth like the sun, wide reaching is his burning
    zeal.

Mary nurtures the Son of tenderness,
God, supreme ruler of every nation:
Her father, her strengthener, her brother.

Mary nurtures a Son on whom dignity rests:
None can violate his boundaries
Whose words are beauty, who is neither young nor
    grows old.

The unwise can never perceive
How Mary is related to God:
Her Son, her father, her Lord.

But I know, though I be but frail and earthly,
How Mary is bonded in the Spirit to the Trinity:
Her Son and brother in the flesh,
Her father, her Lord, blessed almighty.[11]

For all its simplicity the poem is carefully articulated poeti-
cally and theologically. It has its biblical reference; when, for
instance, we are told that Mary's Son 'goes forth like the sun',
we are almost certainly meant to think of the verses in Psalm
19 which were frequently used, in the early centuries, of the
incarnation; they speak of the sun 'which comes forth like a
bridegroom out of his chamber and rejoices like a champion
to run its course . . . nothing is hid from its burning heat'
(Psalm 19:4, 5). Again, in verse three of the poem we can see
a conjunction between the themes of strength and tenderness
which often characterises praise of the Christ child.

The poem is not addressed to Mary but it contains a sustained reflection on her place in the scheme of redemption. Throughout, Mary is seen in relation to her son, seen as the one through whom and in whom the incarnation of the Word takes place. There is nothing of sentimental piety here, but rather a deeply felt theological wonder before the divine condescension implied in this birth. The poet himself steps into the poem in order to emphasise his sense of awe and unworthiness before this mystery.

In the last verse the trinitarian intention of the whole text becomes explicit. The second line, translated literally, speaks of Mary's bond to the 'spiritual Trinity'. The adjective 'spiritual' here needs to be given its full weight. It is in and through the work of the Holy Spirit that Mary is related to the Trinity. It is in the Holy Spirit that Christ is conceived in her womb, it is in the Holy Spirit that Christ's birth is made known in the church, and understood insofar as it can be understood. This birth is of universal import. Christ is to be born in the heart, in the centre of the being of all who believe. What is true of Mary, in a unique and original sense, consequently becomes true of all those who believe; in them too Christ is to be born through the power of the Spirit.

It is the trinitarian quality of the work that is most striking. It is not only in the Spirit that Mary's child is conceived. It is in the Spirit that she is now bonded with him. All the paradoxes of faith come into play here. He who is her Son is also her father and her Lord; he is at once her Son and God's Son.

There is something very thought-provoking in the fact that the Welsh tradition of theological praise poetry begins with these two texts which link together so closely the two basic doctrines of the Christian faith. When so much of the poetry of these early centuries has been lost, when all that we have are fragments, it is remarkable that these two texts have been

19

preserved for us, poems which bear witness to a direction which will be followed for more than a thousand years.

CHAPTER TWO

Poetry's Welfare Is in Elohim's Care:

The Varieties of Praise

In the first chapter we said that God's presence makes the world. That statement must not be misunderstood to mean that the world is simply passive and inert before the divine action. God creates a world which he endows with life of many kinds, life which is dependent on his life but which has a dynamic of its own. He also endows his creation with freedom of many kinds. In the case of men and women that freedom can rise up into the possibility of conscious co-operation with God. Human beings can share in the creation of the world. All God's theophanies, disclosures of himself, involve an act of self-communication. They thus call out an active response on the part of creation. Creation is summoned to share with God in the power of his creative act, and one of the primary ways in which we may begin to do that is through the practice of praise.

Here as always in speaking about the presence and activity of God, we need to keep in mind the mystery and many-sidedness of the reality of which we speak. As Macquarrie says, 'God is both temporal and eternal. There is a sense in which everything is already fulfilled in him and it is the vision of all things subjected to God, *sub specie aeternitatis*, that has acted as a powerful source of hope and confidence among human beings engaged in the struggle for a better world. Yet,

21

if the struggle is real, it must be real for God too . . . Though the language is certainly bold, it does not seem to me entirely wrong to say, with Eriugena, that God is actually making himself in the temporal world . . .'[1]

God comes out of himself into his world both in creation and redemption. He suffers in those who suffer, taking their pain into himself. He heals in those who heal, in those who show by their own action and suffering that their life is being filled with his divine life. Such a view of the intimacy of interaction between human and divine is implicit in the theology of the early centuries, for instance in the teaching of Maximus the Confessor, the great seventh-century theologian. 'Maximus uses the doctrine of the uncreated energies of God to underline the fact that God holds us all together with himself by reason of his active suffering with all . . . For the energies of God are not shut in on themselves but come out into the world and are active throughout creation.'[2]

Such an understanding and experience of the divine-human interchange is presupposed and reflected in the poems which we shall be considering. God's presence makes the world; all things may be the occasion of his self-disclosure; that means that all things are called actively to respond to his call, to come to life in his life, to share in the generosity of his giving, to rejoice in his joy. This is what we do when we praise him. This act of praise opens out to include all creation but it is focused in the action of humanity. Within the human family it is focused again in the person of the poet, the maker, the carpenter of song, the one who gives voice to the praises of everything that has breath.

I

We see this very clearly in the poem '*Glorious Lord I Give You Greeting*', one of the few poems from this early period which has been widely circulated both in Welsh and in English translation and has found its way into anthologies and into the hymn book of the Church in Wales:

Hail to you glorious Lord!
May church and chancel praise you,
May chancel and church praise you,
May plain and hillside praise you,
May the three springs praise you,
May darkness and light praise you,
May the cedar and sweet fruit tree praise you.
Abraham praised you, the founder of faith,
May life everlasting praise you,
May the birds and the bees praise you,
May the stubble and the grass praise you.
Aaron and Moses praised you.
May male and female praise you,
May the seven days and the stars praise you,
May the lower and upper air praise you,
May books and letters praise you,
May the fish in the river praise you,
May thought and action praise you,
May the sand and the earth praise you,
May all good things created praise you,
And I too shall praise you, Lord of glory
Hail to you glorious Lord.[3]

We have said already that one of the most striking features of the Celtic view of the world as God's creation is the sense of its variety, its diversity. Certainly the early poets of the Celtic world were aware that the foundation of Christian faith contains an affirmation of the unity and coherence of the world seen as the work of the one Father and creator of all. But that unity is not something monochrome; the early

Welsh poets thank God explicitly for having made a world that is not uniform.[4] One of the greatest gifts of the Celtic Christian vision is this perception of the world as alive and growing and infinitely various. It is a view of creation which allows for difference, which sees, as the writer of Ecclesiasticus puts it, that 'all things come in pairs, one opposite the other . . . Each supplements the virtues of the other'.[5]

We can see this clearly in this poem of praise. At first sight it looks almost haphazard in its gathering together of things to praise God, but as we look more closely we begin to see that it has a carefully worked out pattern. Most of the lines contain pairs of things, darkness and light, grass and stubble, male and female, books and letters. Each supplements the virtue of the other. Then we begin to notice that the images themselves have been carefully selected so as to be deliberately inclusive of the many elements within creation. There is the world of nature with small things and great things, the sand and the earth, the seven days and the stars. There is the world of living things, plants and trees, the fish in the river. There is the world of human life, thought and action, books and letters. There is the history of God's dealings with his people in the old covenant, Abraham, Aaron and Moses; there are his dealings with his people in the new covenant in church and chancel.

At the end of the poem the poet, the singer, himself stands out, 'And I too shall praise you, Lord of glory'. As we shall see time and again these acts of praise are at once universal and particular, involving the whole creation, yet the work of one person, uttered by a single voice which has the task of speaking on behalf of all.

We can also see in this poem some of the characteristics of Welsh poetry, which are evident already in this early period and are evident too in the highly developed verse of the high middle ages. The images are sharp and clear and are carefully

24

ordered. They are ordered, however, in a way which sometimes seems to us random and arbitrary. The outlines of the
poems are sinuous and sometimes irregular. They remind us
of the supple lines which link up the different elements of the
great illuminations in the Celtic manuscripts of Britain and
Ireland.

Writing of the literary quality of this poetry, Tony Conran
says, on the basis of his long knowledge of it as a translator,
'It involved the clear delineation of the image, albeit in a
fashion strange to the English mind. The technique was
impressionist, in that they used no modelling or perspective.
The background and foreground were joined in a pattern of
word-play, similar to the brushstrokes of a Cezanne or a Van
Gogh. Images were used glancingly, not carefully placed or
composed in fixed relation to one another. The brilliant
texture of these poems is not a fortuitous "extra", it depends
for its effectiveness on a mosaic of themes which together
build up a central unity.'[6]

We have seen this unity in diversity in a poem that contains elements which remind us of the praise poems to be
found in the Old Testament psalter. We can see the same
quality in another poem, explicitly in praise of the Trinity,
which even in translation, seems to dance its salutation to the
Almighty:

> I praise the threefold
>   Trinity as God,
> Who is one and three,
> A single power in unity,
> His attributes a single mystery,
> One God to praise.
> Great King I praise you,
> Great your glory.
> Your praise is true;

I am the one who praises you.
Poetry's welfare
Is in Elohim's care.
Hail to you O Christ,
Father, Son
And Holy Ghost,
Our Adonai.

I praise two,
    Who is one and two,
Who is truly three,
To doubt him is not easy,
Who made fruit and flowing water
And all variety.
God is his name as two,
Godly his words,
God is his name as three,
Godly his power,
God is his name as one,
    The God of Paul and Anthony.

I praise the one,
    Who is two and one,
Who is three together,
Who is God himself.
He made Mars and Luna,
Man and woman,
The difference in sound between
Shallow water and the deep.
He made the hot and the cold,
The sun and the moon,
The word on the tablet,
And the flame on the taper,
Love in our senses,

> A girl dear and tender,
> And burned five cities
> Because of false union.[7]

The poem is wholly taken up into the praise of a God in whom unity and multiplicity are paradoxically combined, who is at once one and many, whose life itself overflows into a creation which is also one and many. As we have already seen, the poet is vividly aware of his own unique part in this whole action. He underlines it in the first verse and he comes back to it in the last, when having spoken of sun and moon, man and woman, he suddenly homes in on his own immediate surroundings, the flame on his taper, the word on his tablet. In the first verse he stresses too the importance of poetry itself in the work of God, the *opus Dei*. 'Poetry's welfare is in Elohim's care.' God is concerned about the use of words, for they are vital to the living of human life and the creation of human society. Above all he is concerned about the use of the words which articulate the sacrifice of praise and thanksgiving.

There are many signs in the poem of the poet's theological acumen. In verse two, for instance, he first praises God as two, godly his words; we are reminded that the second person of the Trinity is God the Word. He then praises God as three, godly his power; we are reminded that the third person of the Trinity is the Spirit, the life-giving power of God. He praises God as one, and we are astonished to find a reference to Paul and Anthony. This is not the apostle Paul, but Paul of Thebes and Anthony of Egypt, two of the founding fathers of Christian monasticism, two of the first hermits who lived a life of solitude and silence.

It is Kierkegaard who tells us that 'purity of heart is to will one thing'. The hermit embodies that purity of heart, that singleness, that one-pointedness. He or she images in their life the unity of God. But by a wonderful paradox, the one who lives alone is at least at times called to moments of intense communion with others. So the story is told by Jerome, of the meeting of Paul and Anthony at the end of their lives, spending a day together in thanksgiving and remembrance before God. It becomes one of the foundational stories and images of the Celtic Christian world. We find it referred to here, at a crucial point in this remarkable poem. We find the scene powerfully depicted on more than one of the high crosses in Ireland and on the Ruthwell Cross in southern Scotland. It is one of the few non-biblical scenes to be depicted on them.[8]

The third verse of the poem is particularly devoted to the thought that in creation all things come in pairs, the one supplementing the virtue of the other. Mars and Luna may refer to the planet and the moon or, more probably, to the days of the week, for in Welsh as in French Monday is named after the moon and Tuesday after Mars. Clearly, in this verse, the polarity of male and female is strongly present, and it is in this context that the poet recalls the Genesis story of the five cities of the plain which were destroyed on account of false union. There are, he is telling us, within the overflowing diversity of creation, underlying structures which demand to be respected.

This sense of the multiplicity of creation is to be found in many different forms. In one poem it is linked with a very full affirmation of the place of water among the elements which go to make up the universe. It is very striking that this fluid and elusive element is so highly praised; the structures of the world are not at all static. We also see in this poem another example of the way in which creation and redemption are held together in one. It starts with the thought of the incarnation and it ends with the harrowing of hell. In between it rejoices in the richness of the natural world:

28

Heaven's blessing to creation's fair kingdom
Is the one who comes like a broad-breasted, mighty
   wave.
In every land his name is God,
Mighty flood – Mary reared him.
Well it was that you came in the flesh . . .

The blessing of Heaven's nine ranks on the skilful
   creator
Who caused the light, abundance of joy:
The sun, generous crown of light in the day;
Then the moon, the Christian's candle which shines
   above the sea,
Keeping watch over the peoples of the earth.
The third wonder is the surging of the sea;
Where does the tide turn to? Where does it hide?
The noble Lord has made a fourth wonder;
Flowing fresh water.
Where does it go? Where does it flow? Where does it
   establish itself?
How long will it flow? Or where will it be?
God guides it 'til the seven years of its course are
   complete,
But water never remains where it was.

We beseech the one who creates, mighty God, Son of
   Mary –
When on Easter night you harrowed hell
All who were there were freed –
Oh Lord of Heaven, may we purchase the kinship of
   your kindly pardon.[9]

II

We have seen in the poems so far examined acts of praise which seem almost to dance with delight. But the events of Good Friday and Holy Saturday are ones which can call out a very different response, a very different kind of praise, whose weight and seriousness responds to the weight of what is there suffered and done. If the three poems we have looked at all show considerable theological insight, we come now to a poem which must surely be the work of a writer who has entered very deeply into the understanding of the Christian scheme of things, one who is a theologian in the truest sense of that word.

It is a poem which begins *Yn enw Domini*, in the Name of the Lord, half in Welsh half in Latin, as if to underline the importance of what is to be said. It goes on to praise God for all that he has done and suffered on behalf of his creation. The movement of the poem is slow and solemn. It insists on the priority of God's action. As a literary craftsman the poet uses many of the terms which were employed in his time in the praise of the warrior or prince, as the one who leads his people and defends them from their enemies. But this is no earthly warrior who is celebrated. It is by love that he wins his victories.

> In the name of the Lord, mine to praise, of great praise,
> I shall praise God, great the triumph of his love,
> God who defended us, God who made us, God who
> saved us,
> God our hope, perfect and honourable, beautiful his
> blessing.
> We are in God's power, God above, Trinity's king.
> God proved himself our liberation by his suffering,
> God came to be imprisoned in humility.

Wise Lord, who will free us on judgement day,
Who will lead us to the feast through his mercy and
 sanctity
In paradise, in pure release from the burden of sin,
Who will bring us salvation through penance and the
 five wounds.
Terrible grief, God defended us when he took on flesh.
Man would be lost if the perfect rite had not redeemed
 him.
Through the Cross, blood-stained, came salvation to the
 world.
Christ, strong shepherd, his honour cannot fail.[10]

In considering this poem from the theological point of view we cannot but be struck by the penetration of a writer who, while insisting on the priority of God's work, in creation and redemption alike, also insists on the humility of God's acts. God frees us by his suffering. God's triumph is the triumph of love. The great Pauline theme of the divine self-emptying is given striking expression in the line 'God came to be imprisoned in humility'. The infinite and eternal accepts the narrow limitations of time and space. The source of life becomes vulnerable to human pain and death, enters into the depths of human alienation and loss.

Through this descent into our world God leads us up into the world of his eternal kingdom, into a total liberation from the burden of sin. But none of this is done without cost, without the cost of the five wounds and the perfect act of penitence which only the innocent victim can make. 'Terrible grief, God defended us when he took on flesh.' In the original this line has all the abruptness of the translation. Is the grief ours before the suffering of God? Is the grief God's in the struggle of his passion? Surely it is both.

In the following line we hear of a perfect rite; the original word could also be translated as ceremony. Here surely the author speaks not only of the drama of the cross but of its constant presence now in the sacrament of the altar. In the eucharist the drama is daily renewed through the power of the Spirit in the prayer of the church. There in the presence of Christ the sacrifice which brings us salvation is itself made present and effective. Christ now is the strong shepherd of his people, still their leader and their guide; he still offers himself on behalf of the sheep.

This is a poem which in its solemnity transcends the divisions made by the centuries and by human folly and sin. Although, in terms of style, it could not be further from the verse forms used by Pantycelyn in the eighteenth century in his hymns to Jesus as the conqueror of death, in terms of content there is a strange similarity. Both poets are alike in saying 'Great the triumph of his love', and in understanding the working of that love in terms of the Trinity and the incarnation.

The theme of Christ as redeemer is developed in a number of ways, but always with the thought of the divine-human nature of the one who liberates. He is God, he is man; by his cross, he defends us in this life, he frees us for the life to come. We see this clearly in a Welsh version of a *lorica* or breastplate poem. These lorica poems clearly echo the passages in St Paul which speak of our putting on the whole armour of God (notably Ephesians 6:11–17). They have a firmly biblical basis, but at the same time they take up elements from pre-Christian prayers for protection against evil. The two elements are fused into one, thus giving us another example of the creativity of early Celtic Christianity.

The greatest of these loricas comes from Ireland and is well known through the metrical version made in the nineteenth century by Mrs Alexander, 'St Patrick's Breastplate'. Here is a much smaller version of such a prayer, one which celebrates

Christ in his divinity and in his humanity, which insists on the solidarity of Jesus with the human family and gives a special place to his work as teacher and healer before it comes to ask for the protection of his cross.

On the face of the world
There was not born
His equal.
Three-personed God,
Trinity's only Son,
Gentle and strong.
Son of the Godhead,
Son of humanity,
Only Son of wonder.
The Son of God is a refuge,
Mary's Son a blessed sanctuary,
A noble child was seen.
Great his splendour,
Great Lord and God,
In the place of glory,
From the line of Adam
And Abraham
We were born.
From David's line,
The fulfilment of prophecy,
The host was born again.
By his word he saved the blind and the deaf,
From all suffering,
The ragged,
Foolish sinners,
And those of impure mind.
Let us rise up
To meet the Trinity,
Following our salvation.

Christ's cross is bright,
Shining breastplate
Against all harm,
Against all our enemies may it be strong:
The place of our protection.[11]

III

We began this chapter with a poem which sang the praise of God in and through his creation, and we have gone on to look at a number of poems which praise God as Trinity and praise Jesus Christ as the incarnate Son of God by whose death death has been destroyed. Now at the end we come again to a poem which seeks to express the praise of God through all creation; only this is a longer poem. It is, I would suggest, one of the great religious poems of northern Europe.

The beauty of the virtue in doing penance for excess,
Beautiful too that God shall save me.
The beauty of a companion who does not deny me his
   company,
Beautiful too the drinking horn's society.
The beauty of a master like Nudd, the wolf of God,
Beautiful too a man who is noble, kind and generous.
The beauty of berries at harvest time,
Beautiful too the grain on the stalk.
The beauty of the sun, clear in the sky,
Beautiful too those who pay Adam's debt.
The beauty of a herd's thick-maned stallion,
Beautiful too the pattern of his plaits.
The beauty of desire and a silver ring,
Beautiful too a ring for a virgin.
The beauty of an eagle on the shore when the tide is full,

Beautiful too the seagulls playing.
The beauty of a horse and gold-trimmed shield,
Beautiful too a bold man in the breach.
The beauty of Einion, healer of many,
Beautiful too a generous and obliging minstrel.
The beauty of May with its cuckoo and nightingale,
Beautiful too when good weather comes.
The beauty of a proper and perfect wedding feast,
Beautiful too a gift which is loved.
The beauty of desire for penance from a priest,
Beautiful too bearing the elements to the altar.
The beauty for a minstrel of mead at the head of the
    hall,
Beautiful too a lively crowd surrounding a hero.
The beauty of a faithful priest in his church,
Beautiful too a chieftain in his hall.
The beauty of a strong parish led by God,
Beautiful too being in the season of paradise.
The beauty of the moon shining on the earth,
Beautiful too when your luck is good.
The beauty of summer, its days long and slow,
Beautiful too visiting the ones we love.
The beauty of flowers on the tops of fruit trees,
Beautiful too covenant with the Creator.
The beauty in the wilderness of doe and fawn,
Beautiful too the foam-mouthed and slender steed.
The beauty of the garden when the leeks grow well,
Beautiful too the charlock in bloom.
The beauty of the horse in its leather halter,
Beautiful too keeping company with a king.
The beauty of a hero who does not shun injury,
Beautiful too is elegant Welsh.
The beauty of the heather when it turns purple,
Beautiful too moorland for cattle.

The beauty of the season when calves suckle,
Beautiful too riding a foam-mouthed horse.
And for me there is no less beauty
In the father of the horn in a feast of mead.
The beauty of the fish in his bright lake,
Beautiful too its surface shimmering.
The beauty of the word which the Trinity speaks,
Beautiful too doing penance for sin.
But loveliest of all is covenant
With God on the day of judgement.[12]

A poet of our own century, Waldo Williams, says of the work of praise that 'it recreates an unblemished world'. This is exactly what this poem does, it gives back to us a whole world, remade, restored to its original goodness. It celebrates the beauty and joy of life in this world, a world seen as shot through with the energy and vitality of God. It sees the world as transfigured, as though the poet were looking at it with eyes rinsed and cleansed. But the poem begins and ends with the thought of repentance and penance for sin. Penitence was a major theme in the Christianity of the Celtic world and we are often frightened by the austerity and extremism which for them often seems to go with it and by our own fear that repentance and penance must be actions laden with guilt and feelings of remorse.

We have to recognise that in the first millennium of the Christian era precisely the reverse was the case. The sorrow of repentance was experienced as something full of the potential of life and freedom. This sorrow in the early Greek spiritual writers (*Penthos*) is a sorrow which brings joy (*Charopoion Penthos*). How this was done, how this was experienced is not something we find it easy to understand. To the fact that it was done this poem itself bears eloquent witness. Repentance here is lived as a renewal of baptism, as a God-given way of deliverance from the power of evil and as a God-given way into new life and new freedom.

The second thing to notice about the poem is that like 'Glorious Lord' it seems at first to collect together a great jumble of beautiful things, natural objects great and small, human pleasures and human duties, the vitality of birds and animals, especially horses. In the midst of this celebration of the goodness of life there are a number of lines, not very many, which speak specifically of what we should call 'religious' activities; asking for penance, bringing gifts to the altar, celebrating the ministry of a priest in his church and the beauty of a parish led, not by the priest, but by God. These lines come at the exact centre of the poem and this in itself suggests that they require special attention. They reinforce what was said in the beginning and what is said at the end. Certainly this is a poem in praise of this world and of the life which we are given to live within it. But its vision of time involves a vision of eternity as well. It is held together by a vision of covenant with God on the day of judgement. Grace and nature, sin and forgiveness, time and eternity, earth and heaven are held together in a single perspective.

With a poem of this calibre and this magnitude one cannot but ask what were the circumstances in which it was written and what was the original situation in which it was presented and heard? One thing is certain; such works were not written to be read quietly in private; they were written to be performed in public. But what was the setting for its recitation or singing, the church before or after mass, or the great hall of the prince or bishop? Was it linked to the praise of the liturgy or to the praise of the prince? And who was its writer?

On the one hand its emphasis on repentance and its theological assurance might suggest a monastic origin. On the other hand its delight in human love, its insistence on the prowess of the warrior, in particular perhaps its stress on the value of horses, suggest a more secular background. In fact, in literary terms, the poem has more than a little in common with the twelfth-century poems of 'boasting', *gorhoffedd*, poems in which the poet, in the person of a young warrior, exults in the beauty of summer, in his skill as a warrior and a horseman, in his victories in battle over the English and above all in his victories in love. These poems, for instance that of Hywel ap Owain Gwynedd or Gwalchmai ap Meilyr are among the most attractive of the works of the *Gogynfeirdd*. Here we have a piece which in its delight in the world shows interesting parallels with them but which unlike them, is explicitly anchored in the praise of God and in the life of the church.

For myself I would suggest that the poem is perhaps older than some scholars have thought. It seems to me to date from the period before 1150, before the breakdown of the old Celtic monastic tradition. It speaks out of a society in which lay life and monastic life were still very closely related. The writer's position certainly seems to be that of the layman and not of the priest. The poem speaks of asking for penance from a priest, it looks toward the faithful (in the original 'catholic') priest at the altar. But if the writer is a layman he is actively involved in the prayer and worship of the church. The line which speaks of bringing gifts to the altar is particularly significant in this connection. It points to a time in which the laity were still directly involved in the action of the liturgy, before they had become spectators as they were by the end of the middle ages, even if devout spectators of the celebration of the mass.

What is certain is that the poem reveals, in an extraordinary way, the unifying power of praise. It is uniting for the poet himself. As Tony Conran says on the basis of his own experience both as a translator of such poetry and as a poet, writing on the same principles, 'It gives one a criterion of whole speaking, making poetry as a private person, as a social being and as an objective observer, all at once'.[13] This gift of whole-speak in the use of praise is also noticed by Bobi Jones who himself approaches the question both as a scholar and a poet. In his recent and invaluable book *Cyfriniaeth Gymraeg* he speaks eloquently of the way in which in the work of Pantycelyn one sees how the gift of praise unites in the singer the capacity for love, the capacity for knowledge and the capacity for action in the world.[14]

We are touching here on ways of life and understanding which bring together the different potentials of men and women in ways which our fragmented age often finds it difficult to credit. We are seeing something of what Coleridge called the 'esemplastic' power of the imagination, the power that is, to bring things together into one, a gift of the imagination especially made evident when it is used in response to the esemplastic initiatives of the Spirit.

God's presence makes the world precisely by drawing out in the world the latent capacities of creativity which God has placed there. Within the created and potentially creative world, human beings have a particular place and calling and within the human family the poet, who is not by chance called a maker, has a particular place and calling too. This is the calling of drawing into one things in all their diversity, without that diversity losing its uniqueness and difference. In this act of making we discover what Richard Hooker is pointing to when he speaks of 'the beautiful variety of all things in their manifold yet harmonious dissimilitude'.[15] The world shines out in its first clearness, in that light in which God saw all that he had made and found it was very good.

CHAPTER THREE

The Dawn of Every Altar:

The Abundance of the Middle Ages

The century and a half between 1130 and 1282 constitute a fairly well-defined period in the history of Welsh literature. It is the period of the *Gogynfeirdd*, the rather early poets, as opposed to the *Cynfeirdd*, the really early poets, i.e. those of the sixth century. These are the 'poets of the princes', professional poets who accompany and sustain with their praise the last generations of the native rulers of Wales. In the middle of the twelfth century the confusion caused in England, through the reign of Stephen, allowed the Welsh a certain respite from English pressure. For a century and a half the Welsh made a series of attempts to regroup themselves, to adapt their tribal ways to a feudal pattern of society and to strengthen their resistance to the English. During this period the northern kingdom of Gwynedd played an increasingly important role. There were three notable princes: Owain Gwynedd (1100–1170), Llywelyn the Great (1173–1240) and Llywelyn our Last Prince (1225–1282).

This whole movement was brought to an end by the campaigns of Edward I who conquered Wales in the early 1280s and built a series of great castles to ensure the permanence of his conquest. 1282, not 1066, was the date of the Norman conquest of Wales, and the death of the last Welsh prince is commemorated in an elegy which is perhaps the most amazing single poem in the whole of Welsh literature.

This century and a half was also a period in which much was changing in the church; the general effect of these changes was to bring the Welsh church into closer conformity with the rest of Western Christendom. As the old tribal system broke down in society at large, so the Celtic form of monastic life also broke down. Many of the Celtic monasteries, as for instance at Bardsey or Beddgelert, were transformed into Augustinian houses. At the same time Cistercian communities were founded in Welsh Wales which flourished greatly and soon became centres of Welsh cultural and literary life. Attempts to create an independent church province, with its archbishop at St David's were unsuccessful. The four Welsh dioceses were more fully incorporated into the province of Canterbury.

But if in some ways Wales became more obviously part of the Western Catholic world, the inner life of the nation, especially its poetic life, continued to follow its own course. The poets of the princes were, as their title suggests, much involved in the praise of the earthly ruler. They also sang praise to God and to the saints. Indeed as the time went by in this period, they seem to have turned more and more to the praise of God. In the great poetic dynasty of this time, Meilyr Brydydd, his son Gwalchmai ap Meilyr and his sons Elidir Sais, Einion ap Gwalchmai and Meilyr ap Gwalchmai, it is noticeable that the third generation seems much the most deeply involved in odes in praise of God.

Medieval Welsh poetry very seldom tells a story; it usually assumes that the story is already known and simply comments on it. This is one of the difficulties which we encounter in trying to understand it from a great distance away in time. But there is one poem of this period attributed to Elidir Sais in which we have an extraordinary glimpse of military preparations, the gathering of the Welsh forces from north and south in their last overt resistance to the invader and this passage concludes with the reminder of the transitory nature of all life on earth:

> I have seen Llewelyn like Merfyn in his hosts
> And all Wales trooped around him.
> I have seen chiefs of Gwynedd and the south,
> Columns of war assembled together.
> I have seen men in battle, and stallions restless,
> Wine and people and the field of past time.
> Multitudes I have seen and all the time feasting,
> And the world thriving, the jarring of lords.
> With a flick of the wrist, it has all gone by,
> Everyone leaves this transitory time.[1]

I

This period came to a dramatic end in 1282. We can see in the elegy for the last Llewellyn that there were those who felt that the end of the world had come and all had been lost. And yet within fifty years something new and totally unexpected was coming into existence. Tony Conran writes, 'It was hardly, one would have thought, a likely situation for a high culture to flower . . . And yet, within sixty years of the conquest, Wales had produced her greatest poet Dafydd ap Gwilym, and with him a new freedom, a new and splendid imaginative life. For two centuries, she enjoyed an outburst of fine poetry unrivalled for its sophistication, its brilliance and poise, by anything the Celts have ever achieved before or since. Poet after poet, many of them of a standard one must call great, attained to a classical elegance in their art which English poetry can only match in the later years of Elizabeth and the seventeenth century . . . It is as though the cultural forces that had first shown themselves in the art of La Tène and had been fused with Roman and Christian motifs in the culture of early Ireland and Northumbria, had now at last, after terrible setbacks all over their field, come to fulfilment in the poverty stricken uplands of occupied Wales. The Welsh poets expressed and enacted in their poems a civilisation essentially Celtic, however influenced by accidentals from outside; . . . that is to say their work defined a way of looking at things, proper to full humanity, in which men could be free to develop as individuals within the context of a way of life they felt to be good.'[2]

That civilisation was still not based in cities. There were none. The nearest thing to a large town was Oswestry on the English border. It is a striking fact that in Welsh today the words for civilised and civilisation have nothing to do with urban living. *Gwar* and *gwareiddiad* come from a root which means warm and welcoming and they have come to mean gentle, kindly, courteous and generous. Civilisation is a quality to be found in a farmhouse as much as in a city square.

This medieval culture, praised by the poets, was based in the manor houses of the gentry. There the whole Celtic tradition of hospitality and social life flourished. It was a life in which poetry and music had a privileged place and it was this life of the great houses which the poets of the fourteenth and fifteenth centuries loved above all to celebrate. We can see certain parallels to it in Chaucer and perhaps more closely in the writings of the Gawain poet, for he comes from Cheshire, a part of England not far from Wales and more closely allied to it culturally than the metropolitan south-east to which Chaucer belongs. But what was the part of religion in all this?

Let us plunge straight into a poem from the latter part of the fourteenth century, celebrating the hospitality to be found in the household of John Trefor, the Bishop of St Asaph. The poet, Iolo Goch, is one of the outstanding poets of his time, a man who sings the praises of the Welsh nobility and indeed of King Edward III himself. In the poem which we shall examine, the poet is an old man enjoying the bishop's hospitality. The poet's link with the bishop is clearly a close one, and this is not surprising since John Trefor was the only bishop of his time in Wales to be a native Welshman, one who cherished the traditional ways of Celtic hospitality. As R.R. Davies remarks, 'The two odes addressed to him by Iolo Goch show how much the success and munificence of a native born bishop could restore heart to Welsh society.'[3]

In the poem Iolo speaks of himself as 'a thoroughly joyful *Llywarch Hen*'; *Llywarch Hen, llawen oll*. Llywarch Hen is a figure who appears in the saga poetry of the tenth century. He is the very type of the old man, who is anything but joyful; he mourns the passing of the years, the loss of his faculties, above all the death of his sons killed in resisting the English invasions. Here, on the contrary, is an old man who can rejoice![4]

The poet opens with praise not only of the bishop and his fellow guests, but of no less than eleven members of the bishop's household, many of them, as we shall see, quite low down on the social scale. He greets them all; and if we suppose that the poem would have been recited aloud before the household on some major feast, perhaps during the twelve days of Christmas, we can imagine the characters mentioned in it hurrying into the great hall from outside, to register their unexpected mention in the work of the poet.

He begins, as we have said, with a greeting to the bishop himself and to his distinguished visitors, clerical and lay, 'Scholars, readers of books, squires and nobles,' and then he comes to particulars:

To his chamberlain
That man of all the handful is my soul,
And the chief cook, he was found preparing,
And the well dressed doorman,
And the pantler and the little butler –
My Lord was there ever a kinder man? –
The baker, the beerman the third turn,
The cater – may God keep him –
And the man who dispenses oat fodder and the best hay
To the men and to their horses,
And the man for me, don't interrupt my words,
Who out of respect opened the gate.

Does the parenthesis in the last line but one suggest that the poet was aware that he might be interrupted by applause and laughter at the mention of such a variety of people? Having enumerated them all, there follow some of the most important and fascinating lines in the poem:

I was their dear, their good companion
Keeping the festival with them
A thoroughly joyful Llywarch Hen
Coming and going as I please.
My situation is good, it is no weak invitation
To be here in winter with Ieuan.
Health and life to the man.

Medieval society was strongly hierarchical. Everyone knew his place. Yet within such a system surprisingly free and confident relationships are possible. I remember the way in which forty years ago, the country people on a Greek island would come and greet the abbot of the monastery where I was staying. They would touch the ground with their hand, in a deep bow, before kissing the abbot's hand; then they would rise and speak to him with a freedom and frankness which is not always to be found when dealing with people in official positions in our own more outwardly egalitarian society. Here in this wealthy and in some ways worldly bishop's household in the late fourteenth century, the poet can still say of all these people 'I was their dear friend, their good companion, keeping the festival with them'. In the feast of Christ's birth, in the presence of God, all are made one.

The poet goes on to describe his day. Remember that this is a bishop's household:

> I knew when I met him
> In the courtyard . . .
> I would be welcomed dearly
> And receive his blessing . . .

Twice, no, sometimes three times in the day, he receives the bishop's blessing. Then comes:

> A great delightful brilliant mass
> And that fully sung
> Mean, treble, quatreble and constant bourdon,
> Keenness of repentance and beauty of music.

Was this in the nearby cathedral, we wonder, or was it in the bishop's chapel? After mass he goes to the great hall, where he is placed at the high table, receives the same dishes, yes, and the same wines as his host. But then his host is the soul of generosity.

The hall is not only for eating and drinking.

> I would get poetry, eloquent, full of longing,
> The splendour of the heart's music,

Pleasant clear sweet harmony,
And there would be pipes and dancing every day.

Then he is invited to visit all the different departments of the
house:

He does not hinder my coming and going
Slowly and unhurriedly.

He goes to the kitchen, then the pantry and the buttery:

When it is cold
I have a turf or log fire,
None of your dumb sea coal here.

In the bishop's own room he is entertained with special deli-
cacies and in the chamberlain's quarters there is leisurely chat:

And good free-flowing liquor
From my Lord's drinking horns,
Kept in a case.

The sleeping arrangements are no less comfortable. Indeed
the visitor has all he needs from the hand of this generous
lord:

Gentle, kindly companion,
Lord of shining rank,
Lord of the monastic community.

Here almost at the end of the poem we have lines which sum
up the poet's complex attitude towards his host. He is a gentle
kindly companion and he is at the same time a Lord of
shining rank, and also head of the *clas*, the old Welsh word

for a monastic community. In its total fusion of sacred and secular, we might be inclined to say in its total confusion of the two, the household of St Asaph's in 1395 is perhaps not so very different from what a Celtic monastery might have been some seven centuries before.

The way in which, at the end of the poem, the thought of the monastic community emerges explicitly, helps us to recognise the signs of common life latent in the poem as a whole. It alerts us to the poem's suggestion of possibilities of human contact, of mutual respect and affection across social barriers which we could easily suppose impassable in a society as hierarchical as that.

This quality in the poem throws light on another, better-known work of Iolo Goch's. This is 'The Ploughman' in which the poet celebrates the lowest order of medieval society, the labourers in the fields. This is a remarkable poem from many points of view and has no parallel in medieval Welsh. It is a praise poem, not addressed to someone at the top of society but to someone at the bottom. This in itself suggests that it may have a distinct gospel resonance in it. From the literary point of view it is also unusual. It contains, for instance, a long passage of *dyfalu*, in praise of the plough itself. *Dyfalu* is a riddling style, full of extravagant metaphors, often used for satire, but here used altogether affirmatively and with great skill.

Certainly the poet is no revolutionary. Iolo Goch has no desire to overthrow the established order of society which was sometimes threatened in the years of social upheaval following the Black Death. He would have felt little sympathy for the Peasants' Revolt which had taken place in England in 1381. Yet he wants to do justice to the common man and he feels free to criticise, at least implicitly, the violence and the injustice which he sees in the powerful.

The poem begins with the thought of the day of judgement, when all will be summoned before the judge. There, all are on an equal basis. There the ploughman, if he has lived well, will be joyful and confident in his speech before the tribunal. After lines which praise the generosity of the labourer there follow lines which imply strong criticism of many aspects of life in the fourteenth century:

> He'll pass judgement on nothing but ploughs,
> He does not care for quarrels;
> He wants no part of warfare,
> He'll press noone for what's his;
> He'll not treat us harshly,
> He'll drive no unjust demands;[5]

Do we hear in these lines some of the resentment of the Welsh against the English, which was to burst out in the Glyndwr rebellion?

There follows the most crucial statement of the poem; Iolo's 'immortal compliment to the ploughman' as R.R. Davies describes it:

> Without him no life or world.

> *Nid bywyd, nid byd heb ef.*

Again the poet insists on the contrast with the warrior, speaking of the ploughman's peaceable nature and contrasting his actions with those of the greatest of Welsh heroes, Arthur himself, here called 'Arthur the Plunderer', thus reminding us that in Wales there was a distinctly critical tradition about Arthur as well as a highly affirmative one.

But again he comes back to the ploughman.

We'd lack without his labour
Christ's sacrifice, food of faith.

Aberth Crist i porthi Cred.

All Christendom depends on his labour, from pope and emperor downwards.

It is here that we arrive at the heart of the poem. The ploughman, in sowing the wheat which makes man's daily bread, holds up the structure of the world. This is so quite simply because daily bread is essential for life, but also because daily bread finds its final meaning and destiny when it becomes the bread of life on the church's table, making Christ's sacrifice present in the midst of his world. The poet affirms in his own terms and with his own particular insights, the faith asserted by St Paul about the whole body of the faithful. The apparently least honourable members of the body are as necessary to its life as the most honourable ones. Indeed they deserve to be honoured particularly for their role is indispensable. The relation of the eucharist and God's presence in it to the whole structure of the world is again affirmed in a powerful if unselfconscious way.

In speaking of the ploughman Iolo Goch does not have the kind of mystical vision which we find in William Langland, in whose work the ploughman is seen as the type of Christ himself. Iolo, unlike Langland, has not seen society from the bottom up nor does he have his religious intensity of vision. But what is said here, though less original, is none the less impressive. It is part of a whole sacramental way of viewing society and the world. We do not understand the poem if we interpret it primarily or even solely in political terms; its final perspective is theological.

In a seminal article published in the 1920s Saunders Lewis first pointed to this sacramental understanding of the life of society as something assumed in the poetry of this period, and as something essential to any adequate appreciation of it. Speaking in particular of the work of Dafydd Nanmor, he showed how for the poets of this time the great house with its hospitality created possibilities for the growth of human society and human culture.[6] In such poems there are plenty of descriptions of feasting and enjoyment of the finest wines, but that is not all. We find that the house is open and welcoming to beggars, a hospice for the sick, a refuge for the poor. Again the values of the gospel are affirmed.

And these precious human gifts are not enclosed in themselves. They are rooted in realities deeper than themselves and they point to greater realities than themselves, ultimate realities beyond this world of space and time. It is Bobi Jones who points out that there is, especially in Dafydd Nanmor, a particular fusion of earthly and heavenly, of temporal and eternal. These poets bring together into one the different orders of reality, grace and nature, divine and human. The very details of the house, its order and its furnishing, can speak of the generosity of God as well as of the generosity of the householder who is thus God's servant and representative.

The house with its table for shared feasting and shared celebration points us to a house not made with hands, a kingdom in which God and humankind join together in a common feast in which the celebration of time is fulfilled in the celebration of eternity.

II

The presence of Christian faith and devotion in the poetry of this period is, as we have seen, sometimes implicit, and sometimes explicit. The poets of the fourteenth and fifteenth centuries sing poems in praise of God no less than their predecessors have done. This element in their poetry is something which has not yet been fully explored. Some of the basic texts needed for its appreciation have still to be published. Dafydd ap Edmwnd, for instance, is well known as the most accomplished of all the poets of the fifteenth century, the one who established the twenty-four metres still used in strict metre poetry today. What is not so well known is that half his poetic production is still unpublished and that a large part of the unpublished material consists of poems to God and to the saints. In the view of some of those who have examined this writing it seems possible that we shall find the most deeply felt of all Dafydd's poems here. If indeed this proves to be the case it would considerably alter our view of the poetry of this century.[7]

But the greatest of all the medieval Welsh poets comes not from the fifteenth century but from the fourteenth and he is Dafydd ap Gwilym. Dafydd is a man difficult to describe, a man of complex, shifting moods and attitudes, a man full of humour and irony, a humour often turned against himself, 'like all great comics often profoundly sad'. He is a man with an appreciation of the many sides of life. He gives us a glimpse of the life of the towns, of the hospitality of the gentry. He is up to the moment with the latest developments of his century; the first poet to mention the invention of the clock, an instrument he does not care for at all.

Still more he is the poet of the hillsides in summer, the leafy hiding places where he has made his assignation with his latest love, for he is above all the poet of love. Yet this poet of love is also the poet of nature. In his joy in the birds and animals of the countryside, and in the countryside itself, we find one of his most characteristic qualities. This is a quality which has seemed to many to relate him to the earlier Celtic tradition which also sees creation shot through with the light and glory of God. In much of his poetry there is an extraordinary lightness. It is light in the sense that his words seem to dance; it is light in the sense that it is interlaced with humour; it is light in the sense that the summer sunshine seems to glisten through its lines.

Let us look for a moment at a poem in which these things are expressed. It concerns a bird messenger sent by his beloved to carry a message of love. But this device of the messenger seems only an excuse to paint a picture of the woodland in May in terms of the celebration of the church's eucharist:

> I was in a pleasant place today
> Beneath mantles of fine green hazel,
> Listening at break of day
> To the skilful cock thrush
> Singing a splendid englyn
> Of fluent signs and lessons . . .
> It was Morfudd who sent him,
> Foster-son of May,
> Skilled in the arts of song,
> Swathed in the vestments
> Of flowers of the sweet boughs of May,
> His chasuble was of the wings,
> Green mantles of the wind.
> By the great God, there was here
> Only gold for the altar's canopy.
> In bright language I heard
> A long and faultless chanting,
> An unfaltering reading to the people
> Of the gospel without haste,
> And on the hill for us there,
> Was raised a well formed leaf as wafer,
> And the slender, eloquent nightingale,
> From the corner of a nearby grove,
> Poetess of the valley, rings out to the many

53

The sanctus there in her clear whistle
Raising the sacrifice on high
To the sky above the bush
With adoration to God the Father,
And with a chalice of ecstasy and love.
This psalmody pleases me:
It was bred by a gentle grove of birch trees.[8]

What are we to make of such a poem? Is it an illegitimate, possibly blasphemous application of religious language and images to adorn a secular subject? Does it reveal a basically pagan delight in nature, decked out in ecclesiastical vocabulary? Or is it simply a conventional literary form which has parallels in fourteenth-century French? I want to suggest that it is none of these things. Rather it needs to be read against the tradition of writing which we have already been examining, in which creation and redemption, nature and grace are not set in opposition to one another. This is a tradition in which sacred and secular are not held apart, in which to say that God's presence makes the world is not very far from saying that Christ's presence makes the mass. The modes of God's presence in creation and redemption may be very different; the presence itself is one. It is this way of seeing things that lies behind Dafydd's poem.

Is this an excessively theological interpretation of the poem? It is after all a wonderful example of the lightness of Dafydd's vision, its elusive magical quality, in which different levels of meaning shade off imperceptibly into one another, in which we move from grace to nature, from nature to grace within a single line of verse. Do we have to make its religious meaning so explicit? We certainly are under no compulsion to do so. The poem stands in its own integrity and speaks for itself and will certainly say different things to different people. But a theological understanding of it seems not inappropriate, especially when we see it in the context of the tradition from which it comes.

But for its full theological implications to be seen we need also to put this poem next to Dafydd's explicitly religious and theological poems. Of these there are only five. No one could say that they are a dominant element in his work. Yet their authenticity is not questioned and they give us part of the total picture of the man. It is difficult to deny, as Richard Loomis puts it, that they are both 'impassioned and intelligent . . . sacramental yet personal, orthodox yet original, an elaboration prompted by individual feeling of a central theme of medieval belief'.[9]

Of them, the greatest is a kind of meditation on the eucharistic devotion, the *Anima Christi*. It is a sign of Dafydd's extraordinary awareness of new developments in the life of Europe as a whole, for this prayer, which has a continental origin, itself dates from the early fourteenth century. It is astonishing that he should have known it so soon.

> *Anima Christi sanctifa me*
> Renowned, merciful heart of Three In One,
>> Glory of the prophets,
>> Fair soul of Christ of the fair cross,
>> Like a jewel within, cleanse me.

The linking of trinitarian and incarnational motifs which we have seen in earlier poets here comes before us at the outset. The heart of Christ reveals the love at the heart of the Trinity. It is a precious jewel within, within the body of Christ and also within the life of the believer. The poet uses this figure of the jewel to speak of the image and likeness of God, hidden and buried in every human person.

Corpus Christi, salva me
Body of Christ, stricken through hurtful arrogance,
    Flesh that is sought in Communion,
    Cause of salvation, of a pure spirit,
    Because you live, keep me in life.

The body of Christ is the cause of our salvation, the life which is in that body is a life which has gone down into death and which has overcome death. It is the life which can hold us in life, here and hereafter. It is this life which is given us in Communion. 'The body of Christ keep you in eternal life.'

Sanguis Christi, inebria me
Blood of Christ, acting beyond all that is rightly due,
    Lest sadly I be exiled and lost,
    Arise light of God's glory,
    Keep me from the sin of drunkenness.

This is a verse which speaks of various kinds of excess, some destructive, some redemptive and which prays for release from destructive addiction. Christ's life-blood poured out exceeds all calculation of what is right and due. The poet simply puts aside disputes about the nature of atonement. God's love already rises, like the light of God's glory, strong to save.

Aqua Lateris Christi, lava me
Water from the grievous wound of Christ's steadfast
   side
    Blessedly sustaining the cross,
    Divine heart, free from all loss,
    Immaculate circle of life, wash me.

The water which flows from Christ's wounded side is the

source of Christian baptism, the sacrament of cleansing and new life. Here the poet speaks of an immaculate circle of life, taking up the image of the circle, so powerful throughout Celtic tradition as a symbol of what is eternal and divine. This is a fountain of eternal life.

> *Passio Christi, comforta me*
> Passion of Christ of heaven, Lord of the prophets of the world,
>> Severe were your five wounds,
>> Very strong is the true gift of prayer,
>> Great Lord strengthen me.

The suffering of Christ fulfils and sums up the sufferings of the prophets and of men and women of prayer through all the ages. Through these sufferings our prayers are made strong as they could never be of themselves, strong to the healing and relief of a world which itself is trapped in pain and suffering.

> *O Bone Iesu, exaudi me*
> Gentle kind Jesus, turn yourself toward me,
>> Answer of the light,
>> Dawn of every altar of unending praise,
>> Listen, do not condemn me.

Jesus is the answer of the light, the response of God who is light to the darkness of the world. This light is the glory, the dawn of every altar at which the sacrifice of praise and thanksgiving is offered unceasingly. Through the cross a new day, a new dawn begins; all things can be made new.

> *Et ne permittas me separari a te*
> And place me – may mine be perfect victory –
>> By your side, world's Saviour,

> Like the bush, serving with perfect strength
> With endless praise I shall praise you.

The believer is called to be very near to Christ and to share in his victory. He is to become like the bush which burns with the divine presence but is not consumed. He offers the sacrifice of praise with strength given from on high. This note of eternal praise grows stronger, verse by verse. It is to grow throughout eternity.

> *Et cum Angelis tuis lauda te*
> With your hosts of angels mighty Lord,
>> In the light which knows no loss,
>> In heaven it will be made plain
>> How near salvation is. So be it.

Again our nearness to Christ and his nearness to us is underlined. It is this which heaven itself will make clear; how close God has been, how close God is to his creation, through all the vicissitudes of sin and blindness. And this intimate union with Christ which the whole poem proclaims is set in the context of the praise of the angels and the whole company of heaven. In the end we shall see that love was his meaning.

> *Amen.*
> May it be so, may we be brought
>> To heaven's fair kingdom in humble homage,
>> Land of high grace, of long nurturing of grace,
>> Feast of fulfilment, perfect transformation.

The last two lines of the poem are particularly untranslatable:

> *Gwlad uchelrad feithrad faeth,*
> *Gwledd ddiwagedd ddiwygiaeth.*

58

The first word of the last line but one, *gwlad*, land, corresponds to the first word of the last line, *gwledd*, feast. Both land and feast promise us gifts of eternity. The first of the two lines follows the affirmative way. It speaks of a land which is gift, which is grace, which is nourishing, which is lasting. The last line follows the apophatic or negative way. It speaks of a feast which is without emptiness, *ddiwagedd*, which must mean fulfilled. But what is fulfilled? The word is *ddiwygiaeth*. This is the only recorded occurrence of this word in Welsh; it looks as though Dafydd may have invented it for the occasion. It could mean form or perfection, it is also possible that it could mean transformation; it is related to the word for revival or reformation.

I believe that this transformation is what the poet had in mind. He takes up the thought of the previous line which speaks of the long nurturing of grace and carries it further. The feast of the kingdom is no static fulfilment; it is a fulfilment which is always in progress, always going forward. As Pantycelyn was to see four centuries later, the feast of heaven is not the end but always the beginning of song, the beginning of praise. It is an ever new beginning, an ever increasing dawn. The intuition of Gregory of Nyssa, that eternal life is something which is open-ended, an infinite progress into a life which is by definition infinite, comes to new life here.

I do not suggest that we should regard Dafydd as a man of mystical prayer, though who are we to control and allot the gifts of God? I do suggest that a man of his imaginative genius, whatever his mortal weakness, a man who had lived by a tradition which had explored so deeply what is implied in the praise of God, would have been acutely aware of what the terms used in that tradition meant and would have felt their meaning with a power which was painful – sorrow and joy at once. To express what he saw, even if only for a moment, he found this word and gave it to us, an enigma and a challenge.

The late middle ages in Wales was a period of great literary achievement and it went on well into the seventeenth century, even though by that time it was in decline. In Wales it was the civil war and the execution of the king in 1649 that finally brought the middle ages to an end. What we have seen in this chapter is merely a glimpse into a whole world of invention and delight.

CHAPTER FOUR

The Feast and the River:

From the Reformation to Methodism

If the twelfth and thirteenth centuries had seen many changes in the religious life in Wales how much more was this the case with the Reformation of the sixteenth century. Both at the religious and the political level there were, it seemed, violent discontinuities in the life of the country. Politically speaking the Acts of Union in 1536 and 1537 brought an end to the old patchwork of marcher lordships and royal counties. The last traces of the Welsh legal system disappeared; the Welsh language was no longer accepted in any official or public business. Politically Wales was incorporated into England. On the religious side there was the break with Rome with all the momentous changes which followed from it; changes in the church's teaching and liturgy, the dissolution of the monasteries, the destruction of altars and images and paintings, the end of pilgrimages which in Wales had remained very popular.

But here again in all the discontinuity there were at least some traces of continuity. Partly this was due to the conservatism and remoteness of many places in Wales. The little hillside church at Patricio, not far from Abergavenny, not only managed to preserve its elaborately carved screen – that happened in quite a number of places – it also preserved three pre-Reformation stone altars, something which was scarcely

61

ever the case in England. In the Berwyns at Pennant Melangell, the saint's shrine was of course dismantled and the pilgrimage came to an end. Pieces of the shrine, however, were carefully preserved and in the course of the next two hundred years were built into prominent places in the church's structure. The result is that in the last forty years it has been possible to reconstruct the romanesque shrine in something like its original form.

Such signs of continuity are not only the result of remoteness. It soon became clear in Wales, no less than in England, that the reformers were going to divide into two main schools of thought, schools which in the end were to lead to further schisms in the church. On the one side were the radical reformers, who wanted to make the Bible's authority paramount in all matters and to reorder church structures strictly according to the pattern worked out in Geneva. On the other side there was a more moderate party and they were certainly the majority in Wales. They too recognised the supreme authority of the scriptures in matters of faith but they stated their authority more cautiously. What cannot be proved from scripture may not be required as necessary for salvation; but on other matters, and they were not necessarily trivial ones, the authority of the church to make decisions was recognised.

That meant the church of the past as well as the church of the present was to be considered. The pre-Reformation centuries were not altogether forgotten and set aside. To understand the scriptures rightly this school of thought became more and more convinced that we need to understand them in the light of the tradition and particularly in the light of Christian tradition of the first centuries. So in the Anglican theology of this time the fathers of the church were given an authority second only to that of the Bible.

Another of the ways in which this division showed itself already in the 1580s concerned attitudes to the Church of

Rome. Was it a church at all, or was it simply a synagogue of Satan? Or was it truly a church, even if one seriously in need of reformation? There was no doubt where the parties stood on this issue and to them it seemed one of paramount importance. It determined how they should regard their pre-Reformation fathers and mothers in the faith. Were they necessarily consigned to damnation? Or were they, despite the differences, joined to us in a common faith?

This question is not at all irrelevant to the subject of this book. Its subtitle speaks of the Celtic vision through the centuries in Wales. Was there, we must ask, any continuity of that vision, through the period between the Reformation and the twentieth century? Did people continue to have a sense of indebtedness to their predecessors? It is not always an easy question to answer.

If we take one of the salient points in the twentieth-century understanding of Celtic Christianity, the doctrine of creation, it might well seem that there was a complete break. The Celtic Christians of the classical period had seen God at work throughout creation and had praised him in and through all his works. The religion of the Reformation, on the other hand, seemed to concentrate almost wholly on the doctrine of redemption through the death of Christ. Creation was not much spoken of, the world was regarded primarily as a temptation; there was a growing tendency to start theology from the fall of man and the doctrine of original sin, not from God's creation of the world and its original goodness as created by him. There was so much stress on the question of *how* God saves us, that the question *for what* he saves us fell into the background. Easter Day was overshadowed by Good Friday.

If we look at the hymns of Pantycelyn and his contemporaries at the end of the eighteenth century we find in them a great emphasis on the cross and a constant exhortation to

Christians to renounce the world as a snare and a delusion. They seem to present a wholly different vision of the faith from that which is generally understood today as Celtic Christianity.

The contrast certainly is a real one but I shall hope to show, particularly in this chapter, that it is easily exaggerated. There is more in common between the two viewpoints than we might at first suspect. In the seventeenth century itself there was a kind of underground ecumenical movement, books of devotion from one side of the divide were adapted and translated by the other. There were Protestant teachers who could stress the importance of finding God in and through his creation as well as beyond it. There were books which presented authentically Catholic elements of the faith as well as authentically Evangelical ones. The sense of continuity which is such a strong feature of the Welsh literary tradition had its influence in religious and theological matters too.

I

In Wales, in the Reformation period itself, the middle position was represented by a number of distinguished churchmen who stood out both as scholars and teachers. Among them were the two bishops most responsible for the translation of the Bible and the Book of Common Prayer, Richard Davies and William Morgan. As has constantly been stressed, the translation of the Bible, completed in 1588, was of vital significance in securing the survival of the Welsh language. It is less often noticed that the translation of the Prayer Book was at the time, perhaps, of even greater importance. Most people could not read and the first editions of the Bible were large and expensive. The publication of the Welsh Prayer Book in 1567 meant that everywhere in Wales where there were Welsh-speaking congregations, the liturgy was celebrated in the language which the people understood. It was this use of the literary Welsh of the Prayer Book, week by week, throughout the principality, which preserved the public status of the language at a time when all other official uses tended to be forbidden.

Theologically speaking, the use of the Book of Common Prayer did more than anything else to maintain a sense of continuity in the church's life and worship in a period of much discontinuity. It is true that the services were now in the vernacular and that ceremonial was drastically simplified. But the presence of the daily offices of morning and evening prayer, adapted from the pre-Reformation offices, the provision for the celebration not only of baptism and communion, but of other sacramental rites, the retention of the feasts and fasts which make up the church's year, all these things were signs of a continuity with the church before the Reformation. It was for this reason that almost from the beginning of the Reformation they were constantly criticised by the more radical reformers. The outstanding statement of the middle or Anglican position, Richard Hooker's *Laws of Ecclesiastical Polity*, grew directly out of the controversy about the Prayer Book.

In Wales the Book of Common Prayer was supplemented, early in the seventeenth century, by a metrical version of the psalms which came to be very widely used and was often bound up with the Prayer Book. It was the work of a scholar and a poet of outstanding ability, Edmwnd Prys, a translation of a quality unparalleled in England. In it we can see the beginning of vernacular hymnody in Welsh.

It is interesting to notice, in the work of Edmwnd Prys, clear signs of his position on the controversial issues of the day. To him the pre-Reformation tradition of the church is of considerable importance. In the debate which he had with William Cynwal, about the nature and purpose of poetry, for instance, Prys defended his own right to be a poet, despite the fact that he had not had a bardic training, by appealing to priests who had been poets in the middle ages, among them Thomas à Kempis.[1] In an elegy which he wrote for two of his contemporaries, successively bishops of Bangor, Richard Vaughan and Henry Rowlands, he begins quite naturally by comparing them with two bishops of the early centuries in Greece, Basil of Caesarea and Gregory Nazianzen. They also had shared their student years, only in Athens rather than in Oxford and Cambridge.

In an outstanding poem, 'The Ode On Our Redemption', the whole of the first part of the poem is devoted to the story of the annunciation, centred on the figure of Mary. Mary is not invoked; she is certainly praised. This leads us on to the second part which celebrates the uniqueness and sufficiency of Christ's sacrifice on the cross. Here we can see polemic on both sides; as against Rome the poem stresses the uniqueness of the sacrifice, as against the Puritans it insists that we rightly celebrate the feast of Christmas, a feast which it emphasises is duly ordained, authorised first by the church in the fourth century and of course nowhere mentioned in the Bible.

Directly relevant to any study of the Celtic element in the Welsh tradition is a remarkable poem of his written in praise of spring. The form and style of the poem is anything but traditional in terms of Welsh verse. It follows the model of an Italian madrigal. But the content of the poem with its delighted celebration of the countryside in springtime, with its birdsong, its flowering trees and its flowing streams reminds us of much which is common in the middle ages. The poem ends with an affirmation of the goodness of this world and the appropriateness of using Sunday for recreation as well as worship. This again was a point of sharp contro-

versy already in the 1580s, and we are left in no doubt of Prys'
position on the matter.

> Good for all is consolation,
> Good for maidens' merriment,
> > Sunday is good for all men;
> This is fair, a joy for age,
> Fair for growth, not trouble,
> > The fresh and flowering meadows.
> Fair the ordering of God the Father,
> > His gift, his manifest grace,
> Fair each voice, fair each turn
> Wherever there's no sin.
> > On the earth
> > So kindly,
> > > Early on the crops,
> > On the groves
> > So gentle
> > Where God's great blessing's given.[2]

A younger friend and neighbour of Edmwnd Prys in
Merionethshire, was a man who though not a poet was
perhaps the greatest scholar of the Welsh language in this
period, Dr John Davies, of Mallwyd. It was he who made the
final revision of the Welsh translation of the Bible and
the Book of Common Prayer for the edition published in
1620. He was the author of what became the standard Welsh
grammar and the compiler of a three-way dictionary – Latin,
Welsh and English. Much of the work of John Davies was in
the copying of medieval manuscripts both in prose and
in poetry. To men of his kind in the seventeenth century, who
worked unceasingly at this task, we owe much of what has
been preserved of the Welsh literature of the middle ages. On
the basis of their knowledge of the language of the medieval

poets they constructed their own scholarly work and elaborated their own literary style.

What interests us here particularly is his work as a translator. From the Reformation onwards, for two hundred years, a large part of what was published in Welsh was not original material but translation from English, and for the most part translation of books of Christian instruction and devotion. Some of these works were doubtless of little value; others were works of genuine learning and substance. Among them is a book written in the 1580s by an English Jesuit, Richard Parsons, and soon translated into English and adapted for the use of Protestant readers. It is this version which John Davies translated in the 1630s, making of it an outstanding work of Welsh prose, *Y Llyfr y Resolusion*.

Saunders Lewis, in an article first published in 1964, makes much of both the form and the content of this work. He points, for instance, to a majestic passage on the relation of the creator and creation. In it the reader is exhorted to meditate on the greatness and majesty of God; to see God enthroned with the whole creation gathered around him. We are to consider how all things depend on the power and goodness of the Almighty and how God's goodness and power penetrate into all things and assure their continued existence. 'So you must think that God, like a glorious sun, is placed at the centre of all things, and that there come forth from him innumerable rays and streams of virtue to every creature that exists, whether in heaven or on earth, or in the air or in the seas, and to every part of every one of them. From these rays of power and goodness all creation has its life and being . . .'[3]

In such a paragraph one can see how important were the elements of Christian faith which were held in common by the two sides in the Reformation conflict. That God is present in his world and constantly holds the world in being by his presence is something which Catholics and Protestants affirm, and they affirm it in unison with the Christian centuries before them. But they have their own way of making that affirmation, a way appropriate to their own time; and here too the two sides in the Reformation conflict often had much more in common with one another than they were aware of.

In his comment on this paragraph Saunders Lewis remarks on two things, first the quality of theological and indeed philosophical reflection which it implies, and secondly the splendour and vigour of its style. This is the baroque style so beloved of the counter-Reformation. Saunders mentions Rubens and Carravaggio as parallels in the worlds of painting. John Davies, he suggests, has succeeded in transposing into Welsh something of the vision of a Jesuit writer from the heart of the counter-Reformation. He has done this despite the mutual hostility of Rome and the reformers. The rector of Mallwyd, the final editor of the Bible and the Book of Common Prayer, had succeeded in conveying to his readers in seventeenth-century Merionethshire something of the power and excitement of the restatement of the Christian faith which characterised sixteenth-century Rome. It is no small achievement and for Saunders Lewis it has a very particular significance, as pointing towards an as yet unrealised possibility of bringing together different elements in his own inheritance.

II

John Davies' book was published in 1632. Seventy years later, at the beginning of the eighteenth century, another more famous book was translated into Welsh, again by a cleric with a parish in Merionethshire, Ellis Wynne. This time the original came from one of the most renowned Anglican writers of the mid seventeenth century, Jeremy Taylor.

Here we have the interesting case of a work written by an eminent stylist in one language being translated by an eminent stylist in another. The early-nineteenth-century critics considered Jeremy Taylor one of the greatest of all English prose writers. Even today, when his reputation is greatly diminished, the distinction of his style is still widely recognised. He wrote much in the fields of theology and spirituality, and he wrote at length. His sentences are lengthy and luxuriant, his images abundant and sometimes wonderfully contrived.

Ellis Wynne's reputation as a prose writer is more assured; but it is based on a single book, *The Visions of The Sleeping Bard*. This is a free translation and adaptation of a satirical Spanish work by Francisco de Queveda. Both in Spanish and Welsh this work, which contains a series of visions of hell, is marked by a savage irony in some ways reminiscent of Jonathan Swift. It seems a long way indeed from the world of Jeremy Taylor.[4]

In his translation of *Holy Living*, Ellis Wynne in general follows his original quite closely, though he often abbreviates. The numerous classical allusions to writers such as Plutarch and Seneca are omitted. Much of the moral exhortation is adapted to the circumstances of his readers. One whole section on the duties of kings and governors is left out as 'unfortunately irrelevant to the Welsh language'. Where Taylor writes in the first and third person singular, Wynne often uses the second person and addresses his reader directly. The result is to make the whole work more homely, more direct, more down to earth.

In this context some of the more theological sections of Taylor's book stand out even more clearly. The patristic material, as for instance the long prayer from the Liturgy of

St Basil, striking enough in English, is even more striking in Welsh. Striking too are the passages in the first section of Taylor's book on the practice of the presence of God and on our faith in God's presence in his world which underlies that practice.

> God is wholly in every place, included in no place, not bound with cords (except those of love), not divided into parts, not changeable into several shapes, filling heaven and earth with his present power and with his never absent nature. So St Augustine expresses this article. So that we may imagine God to be as the air and the sea, and we all enclosed in his circle, wrapped up in the lap of his infinite nature, or as infants in the wombs of their pregnant mothers; and we can no more be removed from the presence of God than from our own being.[5]

Here, as in Richard Parsons, we have powerful elements of Christian teaching which were not in dispute at the time of the Reformation, elements which we have seen were particularly emphasised in the early centuries of Celtic Christianity. Here also we have a striking affirmation of the motherhood of God, not irrelevant to many of our contemporary concerns. How are we to put this faith into practice? Taylor gives much advice.

> Let everything you see represent to your spirit the presence, the excellency, the power of God and let your conversation with the creatures lead you unto the creator; for so shall your actions be done more frequently with an actual eye to God's presence, by your often seeing him in the glass of creation. In the face of the sun you may see God's beauty: in the fire you may feel his heat warming, in the water his gentleness to refresh you: he it is that comforts your spirit when you have taken

71

cordials: it is the dew of heaven that makes your fields give you bread: and the breasts of God are the bottles that minister drink to your necessities.[6]

One of the things for which Taylor specially commends this practice of realising God's presence is that it strengthens our confidence and joy in him.

> It is apt to produce joy and rejoicing in God; we being more apt to delight in the partners and witnesses of our conversation; every degree of mutual abiding and conversing being a relation and an endearment. We are of the same household with God . . . and if we walk with God in all his ways as he walks with us in all ours, we shall find perpetual reasons to enable us to keep that rule of God 'Rejoice in the Lord always and again I say rejoice.' And this puts me in mind of a saying of an old religious person, 'There is one way of overcoming our ghostly enemies, spiritual mirth, and a perpetual bearing of God in our minds.' This effectively resists the devil and suffers us to receive no hurt from him.[7]

In the translation of this passage we can see how Wynne's Welsh is at times stronger and clearer than Taylor's English. We are of the household of God, says Taylor. Wynne has *cyd-tylwyth*; we are God's family, God's kindred. Wynne makes it clearer that it is in our earthly companions that we are to take great delight, the more we find God in them and them in him. This exercise brings us to *yn gwlwm newydd o anywldra*, a new bond of affection, of intimacy. We are part of the family of earth, as well as of heaven, and God is with us here as well as there.

The same point is made very clearly in one of the paragraphs where Taylor speaks of God's presence within human life as well as in the world around. Here he affirms the indwelling of God the Holy Trinity in the human heart and renews the early Christian teaching about the three altars at which Christ intercedes, the altar in heaven, the altar in the gathering of the church, and the altar in the innermost place of the heart.

> God is especially present in the hearts of his people by his Holy Spirit: and indeed the hearts of holy men are temples in the truth of things, and in type and shadow they are of heaven itself. For God reigns in the hearts of his servants. There is his kingdom. The power of grace hath subdued all his enemies. There is his power. They serve him night and day and give him thanks and praise; that is his glory. This is the religion and worship of God in the temple. The temple itself is the heart of man; Christ is the high priest, who from thence sends up the incense of prayers and joins them to his own intercession and presents all together to his Father; and the Holy Ghost by his dwelling there, hath also consecrated it into a temple; and God dwells in our hearts by faith, and Christ by his Spirit, and the Spirit by his purities; so that we are also cabinets of the mysterious Trinity; and what is this short of heaven itself, but as infancy is short of manhood, and letters of words? The same state of life it is but not the same age. It is heaven in a looking-glass (dark but yet true) representing the beauties of the soul and the graces of God and the images of his eternal glory by the reality of a special presence.[8]

Here as in other such places Wynne translates with precision. The reference to the doxology of the Lord's prayer in the first part of the paragraph comes through clearly. In places indeed he sharpens the outline of what Taylor is saying. A cabinet in seventeenth-century English was a place in which precious things were kept; Wynne translates it as treasury. When it comes to the relation of God's presence now to his presence in eternity he is again clearer and more definite. The same state of life it is, says Taylor. Wynne says simply it is the same life. Already now we live the life we shall live in eternity.

It is not of course suggested that in such passages Jeremy Taylor was in any way directly indebted to early Welsh and Irish sources, and thus was in some way presenting what we might call Celtic Christianity. It is true that during the civil war he lived for some time at Golden Grove in Carmarthenshire and that when he was bishop, during his last years, he was bishop in the north of Ireland. But this does not mean that he was aware of the resources hidden in the Celtic languages. Like almost all his English contemporaries he was wholly ignorant of them.

His sense of the ever present reality of God in the world around us and in the depths of our own being was gained from his profound knowledge of the faith and worship of the church in the first centuries in both East and West. In the passages we have quoted we have seen a reference to St Augustine. There is also a reference to Athanasius on the life of Anthony, and to the teaching of John Chrysostom which lies not far behind the passage on the three altars. It was from such sources as these that he was able to renew, in the polemical atmosphere of the seventeenth century, something of the vision and assurance of an earlier age. This vision and assurance Ellis Wynne transposes into Welsh and in so doing brings Taylor's scholarly erudition into a context in which what is said resonates in unexpected ways and picks up echoes from an earlier time.

III

It may have seemed strange to spend so much time on the seventeenth century when we should have been hurrying on to the eighteenth, to the time from 1730 onwards when the Methodist revival broke out in Wales. It is clear that this revival had an astonishing effect on the life of Welsh society as a whole as well as creating a specifically Calvinistic Methodist movement and denomination. But it is important to register the fact that the seventeenth century was not so barren as it has often been portrayed. Part of the strength of the movement of revival when it came was due to the solidity of the work of preparation which had gone on unwittingly in the previous seventy years.

To write about the Methodist revival in any adequate way would require not just one chapter, let alone half a chapter, but a whole book. This was a time in Wales, even more than in England, when a whole society seemed to be touched by a kind of heavenly excitement. The great figures of the first generation, Daniel Rowland, Howell Harris and Williams Pantycelyn, all deserve particular attention. This is specially true in the case of Pantycelyn, with Dafydd ap Gwilym one of the two outstanding figures in the history of Welsh poetry. That these writers and their contemporaries were none of them consciously 'Celtic' in the modern sense of that word, goes without saying. But like Jeremy Taylor they were many of them deeply rooted in the Christianity of the first centuries, as well as in the Christianity of the Bible. Perhaps it is in their assimilation of this early tradition that we find the basis for such Celtic affinities as they had.

What I intend to do is to look at two of the outstanding figures of the second generation of the movement, who flourished round the turn of the century and who, unlike the founding fathers of the 1730s, came from the north of Wales and not from the south. I shall look first at one of the few scholars of the Methodist movement, Thomas Jones of Denbigh, and then, on the background of his writing, turn to some of the characteristics which distinguish the other great hymn writer of the period, Ann Griffiths of Dolwar Fach.

Thomas Jones of Denbigh is one of the more neglected figures in the history of Wales. Born in 1756, he died in 1820. For our purposes it is important to know that he was a man of much learning, a historian and theologian, as well as a poet both in prose and in poetry. He was a hymn writer though not perhaps among the greatest, but also a poet able to write in the style of the middle ages, being deeply influenced by Dafydd ap Gwilym whose works were published for the first time in 1789. It was Saunders Lewis who remarked that Thomas Jones was a lover of Lancelot Andrewes as well as of Dafydd ap Gwilym, something which certainly marked him out among his fellow Methodists.[9] Bobi Jones alone among our contemporaries does real justice to the intellectual and spiritual stature of this great and attractive man. 'The gospel sounds out like a bell and runs like an unpolluted river through the pages of this great writer', he says in one book, and in another 'he is perhaps our greatest theologian ever . . .'.[10]

In a way which is unusual for an eighteenth-century scholar he had a sympathetic understanding of the poetry of the middle ages and a deep interest in the early history of the church in Britain. For him, in contrast with Jeremy Taylor, the Celtic centuries were not by any means strange and unknown. Being an autodidact, who had never gone to university, he was in many ways remarkably independent of the intellectual fashions of his own time.

I intend to quote three passages taken from material published in his periodical, the *Trysorfa Ysprydol*, between 1799 and 1801, each of which gives us an insight into the mind of this extraordinary man. The first comes from a meditation on creation. It is remarkable, not only on account of its beauty, but on account of the way in which it seems to set aside the dominant scientific and theological views of its time. Its vision of the universe is certainly not that of Newton, nor that of most eighteenth-century theologians. It recalls earlier views in which different levels of being mount up towards God, in which there are different heavens each one of which draws nearer to him. Already, even now, in the lowest of them there is a manifestation of God's joy.

In this sublime and splendid edifice I can see three levels; the first encompasses the birds, the mist and the winds; the second is for the stars; and the third is reserved for the saints and the angels. The first is a court which is open to all; the second is like a temple, in which the candles of heaven burn unceasingly; the third is your holy of holies. In the first there is strife and vanity and unreality. In the second order, purity and peace. In the third there is bliss and glory. We experience the first, perceive the second and believe concerning the third. There is no state of bliss pertaining to the two lower levels: we cannot say that birds or stars enjoy happiness. But in the third level you, O Eternal Trinity, find joy in yourself: and you are the bliss of the spirits whom you have glorified. It is the manifestation of your glory which makes heaven what it is. This is your children's privilege: by perceiving you here through faith they are beginning that perfect heaven, which they will enjoy perfectly when they have a perfect vision of you.

But before we go there, what wonders we behold even in the lowest of the three heavens . . . What myriad of wonders there are on the face of the earth. Look at all the seeds, herbs, plants, woods and fruit. See what variety there is of creatures that move or crawl on the earth. What single one among all of them could we contemplate without seeing the mark of your fingers Oh

God? Air, land and sea, and each one of their unnum-
bered inhabitants: all of these proclaim loudly to us the
power, goodness, and wisdom of the eternal creator.
How blind and deaf we must be, if after all this we
continue without recognising our God.[11]

If we ask ourselves where Thomas Jones found this picture
of a world which is gradually lifted up towards God, a world
in which the divine glory penetrates even into its lowest
reaches, we have only to look back into the picture of the
world common in the centuries before the scientific revolu-
tion. This earlier vision of the natural world as full of God's
glory which he found in the medieval poets and which
strongly influenced his own poetic writings also had its
influence into his writings in prose and particularly into the
poetic prose of a meditation like this. Indeed, perhaps we
might see such a passage as a kind of essay in preparation for
a *cywydd* in praise of God.

In the second extract, which comes from a printed sermon,
we find him writing in a more explicitly biblical style. The
beauty of the language is no less and here we find a wonderfully mature and independent mind which seems as it were
effortlessly to hold together emphases and insights which are
evangelical and catholic. He speaks of the Christian life both
as effort and fulfilment. It is a way along which we travel, but
also a feast in which we already share. While both images
point us towards a fullness which is not yet revealed, both
assure us that already, here and now, God is making that
fullness known.[12]

We notice how he insists that the gospel way involves our
sharing, not only in the promises of God, but in the properties of God, not only in what God has, but in what God is. In
the latter part of the passage we perceive the language of
Christian mysticism. We are to let our whole spirit unite with

the divine Spirit, sharing in a treasure which is nothing less than the life and being of God.

According to the Word of God, the way of the gospel is a highway and a holy way (Isaiah 35:8) and if fools go along it, they will be brought safely to the end of their journey. It is a new and living way (Hebrews 10:20) which gives life to the weak traveller and leads him to the sanctuary. Surely it will be good for the soul to travel on it. It is also a feast, a feast of good things and of pure shining wine (Isaiah 25:6–7). A feast of salvation, a feast of delights, a feast of sufficing. If the veil is taken from your mind, you will find yourself on the mountain of God enjoying his feast. Yes it is the great supper. God himself has prepared it, of his great grace and goodness and to great purposes. By feeding freely on what is provided you will be content to go to your silent resting place singing 'Lord now lettest thou thy servant depart in peace' (Luke 2:29) and with David in his last words 'This is all my salvation and all my desire' (II Samuel 23:5).

Salvation in Christ is a feast and it is also a river; a river of virtue and a river of strength. In it the frail believer has all the promises of God and all the properties of God, all that God has and all that God is, as a living water to quench his thirst, as a strongly flowing stream which carries him on its current to the sea of his endless delight. In a word, here is the complete treasury, the refuge, the tent of meeting, the feast and the river, and whatever else you have need of; 'All things are yours' (I Corinthians 3:24). Through the gospel of God's grace, all the fullness of God is the inheritance of the saints. Well then, hide yourself in it; feed on it – yes, cast your frail, weak vessel into the quiet stream of this blessed gospel. Let your whole spirit unite with it, swim in it, drink from it, take it as your life and your nourishment. In this way you will become one who witnesses with ever growing strength, that it is a sweet savour unto life, that it gives life, a life of grace and of peace, ever sustaining it, making it grow and bringing it to its perfection.[13]

In a passage such as this we are given an affirmation of the nature of life in Christ which transcends the differences of Catholic and Protestant, of East and West. A fullness of faith and experience seems to find expression here which testifies to the depth of Thomas Jones' own life of prayer and tells us much about the whole movement in which he played so central a part. If in the passage just quoted we can hear notes which remind us of the hymns of Ann Griffiths, so too, in the following passage, which speaks of the divine humanity of Christ, we find touches which suggest the background of her own devotion to the Redeemer.

In his intercession for us, as in everything else, Christ is a person beyond compare. There is none like him in heaven or earth. There are in Christ, if I may put it like this, two wellsprings to his love and mercy; one in the divine person, the other in the human nature: he loves us as he is God, he loves us as he is man. He has mercy as God, he has compassion and pity as man. It is in these ways that the infinite draws wonderfully close to us. Love as it is found in God, is a thing too wonderful for us. We are overcome by the extent of its wonders; or perhaps it is that these wonders overpower us with their divinity and majesty. But here is a nourishment which is suitable and close at hand. He who is the God of all perfections is perfect man; he loves us, he has compassion and pity on us as man. We know what that is: in our experience we are with him, close to him.

Just as Christ stands in regard to his people in every close and loving relationship: as father, as brother, as bridegroom, as friend etc., so also he has the feelings appropriate to every relationship. The qualities and feelings which in the human condition are divided, are in Christ all united in one. Jonathan loved David as a friend; Joseph loved Benjamin as a brother; Abraham loved Sarah as his bride; Jacob loved Joseph as a father; Rachel loved her children as a mother; but in Christ all these streams have met together. In him are the love and the feelings of a father, a bridegroom, a friend, and of every relationship; and this without the one hindering the other, or diminishing the other, but all abiding together and working together, gloriously strange and holy, in his human nature.

Therefore he intercedes not as one who is unconcerned about the success of his work, but as a mother for her children, as a husband for his beloved bride, as a friend for his friend etc. He also intercedes for friends who were once enemies, but whom he has made friends through his act of dying for them. And if it has become possible for them to be at peace with God through his death, how much more now that they are at peace, will they be saved through his life and intercession on their behalf.[14]

In such a passage we see something of Thomas Jones' meditation on the Chalcedonian definition of the unity of the two natures in Christ. He makes sense at the practical, personal level, of elements in the classical theology of the early centuries which have often been thought abstract and barren. We also see again his way of holding together things that are considered catholic with things that are considered evangelical.

Here certainly is the Christocentrism of the Reformation. All points to the person of Christ. But this is an inclusive and not an exclusive vision. It is Christocentric not Christomonist. All the diversity of the saints of the Old Testament is seen, as it were, shot through with the light of Christ's humanity, building up our picture of what true humanity should be. And what is said of the great figures of the Old Testament history would be no less true of the great figures of the history of the church. We can see in such a passage a way to reinterpret the doctrine of the communion of saints that would resolve many of the difficulties which have divided Christians from one another on this issue.

Above all in this, as in so much of the writing of this remarkable man, one feels great learning and profound reflection put at the service of the whole people of God, of the simplest and least articulate of his fellow Christians. There is a warmth and humanness here as well as a light and precision in speaking of the things of God, which may remind us of the deceptive simplicity of the writings of a Michael Ramsey.

IV

If the name of Thomas Jones of Denbigh is very little known, even in Welsh-speaking Wales, the same is not altogether true of his contemporary Ann Griffiths. Ann remains a figure vividly remembered in her own world and she is beginning to be recognised outside it. We know that she had met Thomas Jones' friend and colleague, Thomas Charles of Bala. Indeed, as often as she could, she would travel the twenty-two miles across the Berwyn Hills to take her part in the monthly communion services at which he presided and preached. We do not know whether Ann ever met Thomas Jones, though it is perfectly possible that she did. We may, however, be sure that she knew his writings. Few can have read the pages of the *Trysorfa Ysprydol*, with its mixture of theology and devotion, of church history and commentary on current affairs, with more eager attention than the young mistress of the household at Dolwar Fach.

Thomas Jones was a voluminous writer now unjustly forgotten; Ann, by comparison, wrote almost nothing, but she begins to be more widely read. There are her few letters, one of which survives in her own writing, and the texts of the hymns which she had composed. But we have none of these in her own hand. The copies which we have were written down after her death at the dictation of her maid and companion who was a good singer but unable to write. Here we have oral tradition functioning at the beginning of the nineteenth century.

As one becomes aquainted with the hymns and letters of Ann Griffiths one is astonished at the way she seems to write with authority and assurance. This is not only the authority of her own experience and reflection, though there can be no doubt about these, but the authority of the Christian tradition as a whole. Coming to know the history of Welsh Christianity better one comes to see more of the influences which could have helped her to grow so rapidly into a maturity of faith and understanding. Among these influences I believe that none was more important than the writing of Thomas Jones of Denbigh. In him she found a teacher whose work had that combination of warmth and light, of depth and expansiveness which characterise her own very different writings. Maybe, in the coming years, as people look further into the work of Ann, they will be led to discover more of the work of Thomas Jones.

One of the reasons why Ann Griffiths is becoming better

known in the English-speaking world is her evident importance in the work of R.S. Thomas. Her name occurs in a
number of places in his writing, most notably in the long
poem 'Fugue For Ann Griffiths'. Like all of us he is puzzled
by her knowledge.

> Is there a scholarship that grows
> naturally as lichen? How
> did she, a daughter of the land, come
> by her learning? You have seen
> her face, figure-head of a ship
> outward bound? But she was not
> alone; a trinity of persons
> saw to it she kept on course
> like one apprenticed since early
> days to the difficulty of navigation
> in rough seas. She described her turbulence
> to her confessor, who was the more
> astonished at the fathoms
> of anguish over which she had
> attained to the calmness of her harbours.[15]

But it is not the particular ways in which R.S. Thomas
understands Ann which are of such importance. It is rather
his whole attitude towards her, an attitude summed up by two
words from this poem, 'Ann, dear . . .'. There is evidently a
deep feeling of kinship with her and of being her contemporary despite the two centuries which have passed, which
alerts one to being open to possibilities of allusions in other
places in his writing. A Welsh-language poet, T. Arfon
Williams, remarks, 'A fair familiarity with R.S. Thomas'
work might well bring Ann to mind, and a knowledge of
her work would in turn illumine his, perhaps.'[16]

The influence of Ann Griffiths is penetrating into the

English-speaking world in other ways as well. At the end of his first published book of poems, Rowan Williams, formerly professor in Oxford, now Bishop of Monmouth, includes a small group of poems translated from Welsh, among them two by Ann. They are translations unlike any other. They are in one sense very free, 'I have adopted . . .' Rowan Williams writes, 'a style of translation designed to be not at all a literal rendering but an attempt to recreate the progressions of imagery with something of the energy they have in the original.'

But if these translations of Ann are free they are also, in terms of the sense, very close. Ann has here met a theologian as translator and the results are striking; the energy, the strangeness, the abruptness of the original, shines through in an unequalled way.

> Wonder is what the Angel's eyes hold, wonder.
> The eyes of faith too, unbelieving in the strangeness,
> Looking on him who makes all being gift,
> Whose overflowing holds, sustains,
> Who sets what is in shape,
> Here in the cradle, swaddled, homeless,
> And here adored by the bright eyes of Angels,
> The great Lord recognised.[17]

Rowan Williams is a newcomer to the translation of Welsh verse. Tony Conran, whose name we have already met, is one of the most experienced of all translators. He too has worked on Ann, and out of his meditation on her work has come to a remarkable conclusion. In a long interview, recently published, he replies to the question 'What do you see as the major differences between Welsh and English poetry?' with four closely packed pages of response.

At first he is tentative, 'It's extraordinarily difficult to generalise about so long a period . . . The truth is the two poetries are incommensurate with each other . . .' But then gradually he homes in on a conclusion, 'In a curious sense, Welsh poetry is always waiting for something to happen. Praise poetry is a poetry of expectation . . . Celtic culture is often said to be obsessed with the past; on the contrary Welsh poetry seems to me to be almost wholly future-directed.' By contrast English poetry is about the present, 'or the past as re-created in the present'. It is also empirical and individualist in a way quite strange to the Welsh tradition.

And yet . . . the analogy I keep wanting to make is based on the old Catholic idea of the two kinds of Christian life, Martha and Mary in the house of Christ's friends in Bethany. English poetry is Martha, it's like the active life, the life of faith in what you are doing, the life of the present . . . Welsh poetry on the other hand is Mary, it is like the contemplative life, it lives in the hope or despair of what is to come. It's like the life of widowhood, the death or the life-in-death of the body of Christ in the tomb, secret, guarded, unacknowledged in the world.

> Oh my soul look! Chief of kings, Author
> Of peace, he lay in that room,
> The creation in him moving
> And he a dead man in the tomb!
> Song and life of the lost! Most wonder
> Of all to Angels and Seraphim –
> God in flesh, they see him and worship,
> Choirs of them shouting, 'Be unto Him'.

It may seem fanciful – after all a good deal of Welsh poetry is worldly, not to say bloodthirsty and boastful – but there is a sense in which those few precious hymns . . . of Ann Griffiths, the farmer's daughter from Dolwar Fach in Powys – hymns never written down in her life time – represent the culmination of fifteen hundred years of Welsh poetry, the ultimate mystical apotheosis of where it's at.

Tony Conran goes on at once to qualify his judgement. 'You mustn't press the comparison too far. I would not be taken as implying that there's anything mystical or other-worldly, certainly about most Welsh poetry. It's not that kind of critical point I am making.'[18] One can understand the need for such qualifications. The point being made is not a simple one; but the judgement remains and it is a remarkable one. If it says much about the place of Ann Griffiths in the whole tradition of Welsh poetry it says much about that tradition itself, the tradition which is the subject of this book.

As we have seen, Welsh poetry often seems to rejoice in the immediately perceived presence and beauty of the world in which we live. We think of the Loves of Taliesin or the poems of Dafydd ap Gwilym. Yet that immediacy of percep-tion is given in the context of a prayer that looks forward to the day of judgement. Our eyes need to be cleansed by a light from beyond this world before we can see clearly what it is that lies before us. It is God's presence that makes the world and that enables our perception of the world. That presence implies both judgement and mercy, but already now mercy triumphs over judgement. To that fact Ann's hymns bear luminous and powerful witness.

CHAPTER FIVE

Watching Two Worlds:

Waldo Williams, Gwenallt and Gwyneth Lewis

The history of the Welsh language and of the literature which it conveys has, as we have seen, been full of surprises. Who could have foreseen the sudden outburst of poetic energy in the centuries after the disaster of 1282? Who, after the old bardic order had died out, could have foreseen the birth of a new and totally unexpected world of Methodist hymn singing in the eighteenth century? The twentieth century has been no less unexpected. On the one side the number of Welsh speakers has declined throughout this period, until now only about 20 per cent of the population of Wales speak the Welsh language. But, at the same time, there has been an explosion of poetic talent which could only be paralleled in the great age of the fifteenth century.

In the first part of this century three names stand out, T. Gwynn Jones (1871–1949), Robert Williams Parry (1884–1956) and T.H. Parry-Williams (1887–1975). All of them were deeply influenced by the founding of the University of Wales towards the end of the nineteenth century and by the growth of the scholarly and scientific study of the Welsh tradition which developed in the Welsh departments, especially in Aberystwyth and Bangor. These writers had an understanding of the history of the language and the literary tradition, and in particular of its earlier strands, which had not been easily accessible to their predecessors. They had a vision of the meaning of the word Celtic as a term which linked Wales with Brittany and Cornwall on the one side, with Ireland and western Scotland on the other, which in many ways was new.

But they were all, religiously speaking, somewhat typical representatives of the twentieth century. They found that they had outgrown the faith in which they had been brought up. Particularly they had outgrown the piety of Welsh nonconformity. They were not, for the most part, hostile to that inheritance; at times they could look back to it with a kind of wistful nostalgia; but it was no more for them. One can feel in their writing a melancholy which is reminiscent of Thomas Hardy.

They were to be succeeded in the thirties and forties by a group of writers whose religious position was startlingly different. Saunders Lewis (1893–1985), Gwenallt (1899–1968), Waldo Williams (1904–71), Euros Bowen (1904–88), all of them, in their very different ways, wrote out of a deep, if often hard won, commitment to the historic Christian faith. They all therefore felt not only at one with the cultural heritage of Wales, but specifically with the Celtic Christian element within that tradition which we have been examining in these pages. They were not trying, in an antiquarian way, to reconstitute that tradition as though it was something of the past. By their poetic creativity they were witnessing now to its present reality.

This sense of the living presence of the past in their work reveals itself in a powerful awareness of the communion of saints. Gwenallt opens his poem in praise of St David with these lines:

> There is no barrier between two worlds in the Church,
> The Church militant on earth

Is one with the Church triumphant in heaven,
And the saints are in this Church which is two in one.
They come to worship with us, our small congregation
The saints who built Wales on the foundation
Of the Crib, the Cross and the Empty Tomb.[1]

The closeness of the saints can reach across the divisions in Christendom no less than across the divisions of the ages. Waldo Williams, a Baptist by upbringing and a Quaker by mature conviction, writing in the 1940s, twenty years or more before Vatican II had opened up relations between Roman Catholics and other Christians, can praise the forgotten Catholic martyrs of the sixteenth century:

The centuries of silence gone, now let me weave a celebration;
Because the heart of faith is one, the moment glows in which
Souls recognise each other, one with the great tree's kernel at the root of things.

They are at one with the light, where peace masses and gathers
In the infinities above my head; and, where the sky moves into night,
Then each one is a spyhole for my darkened eyes, lifting the veil.[2]

Waldo indeed, in his poems, celebrates not only those of the distant past but those of our own day who have died. He has a wonderful strict-metre poem of tribute to a friend, E. Llwyd Williams, Baptist minister at Rhydaman (Ammanford), and another to his mother, Angharad. These are poems of praise and remembrance which function like icons in the Eastern

Orthodox tradition. They bring before us an image of the loved and known person in which the light of God shines through, transfiguring the flesh, giving us a promise of a unity beyond death. So in his poem to Llwyd he can pray:

> Pure God, Father of light,
> Give back to us your dawn.
> Your glory is your heart,
> Love springs up from your holy root,
> Above our clay your love binds us in one.
> You join us together safely above the fall.
> Dwell in us through this parting
> And bring our journey into the one House.[3]

I

It is these poets, and two of their successors in more recent generations, whom I want to look at in these next chapters. Their affirmation of faith in the triumph of God's life in human life, a life which transcends death, is a very precious gift to us in a century which has, as Seamus Heaney suggests, 'too long and too readily approved of' a very different attitude towards death. This is the attitude summed up, for instance, in Philip Larkin's 'Aubade', a work which impresses Heaney as 'the definitive post-Christian English poem, one that abolishes the soul's traditional pretension to immortality and denies the deity's immemorial attribute of infinite personal concern'.[4]

In the Welsh poets of the mid-century on the other hand, in response to this mood, we have a very special affirmation of the death-defying quality of art. At one level this is quite simply the case because of the situation of the Welsh language itself, which to all appearances and on purely statistical terms is threatened with extinction. But it is also more profoundly the case because these poets are speaking out of a tradition which through the centuries has constantly snatched victory from the jaws of death and which can thus, in our own deeply menaced century, when all things human and vulnerable seem threatened with destruction, affirm with particular authority the deeper and more ultimately enduring reality of joy.

Here the poets of Wales seem to me to have a hidden affinity with many of the poetic voices of Eastern Europe, who also speak from nations whose historic experience has been painful and constantly threatened by destruction. Making his own protest against that same poem of Larkin's, Czeslaw Milosz, for instance, insists 'poetry by its very essence has always been on the side of life. Faith in life everlasting has accompanied man in his wandering through time, and it has always been larger or deeper than religious or philosophical creeds which expressed only one of its forms.'[5]

Here also is an affirmation which these Welsh poets would powerfully support. We have said that in Waldo Williams the sense that the past is present with us, that the forces of life are in the end stronger than death, that we are 'keeping house amidst a cloud of witnesses', applies both to the remote and to the recent past. Let us turn now to a sonnet which he wrote towards the end of his life in which both times are consciously commemorated.

The poem records the memory of a moment during the First World War when Waldo, his parents, his brother and his sisters go out into the winter night from the warmth of their fireside to hear the church bell ringing the New Year in. It is a tiny incident vividly recalled; it comes from a period in Waldo's life, his early teens, when he was given some of those fundamental insights which he lived by for the rest of his days. Forty or fifty years later they were to give rise to some of his greatest and most characteristic poems. The best known of them '*Mewn Dau Gae*, Between Two Fields' springs out of a moment of vision given in the countryside near Llandysilio, in fields farmed by the brother of a school friend, John Beynon. That is a moment of vision given in the midst of the world of nature. Here in this sonnet a similar, if smaller moment is set in the context of the village community, a moment full of human history.

> I am often amazed. What light came from beyond
>> That to his elect ones Christ could reveal
> When life for us was brutal, full of wrong,
>> Made great by neither purpose nor ideal?
> I remember how we'd all go to the door
>> When the church bell rang for a better year –
> Maldwyn's gentleness on Dyfed once more,
>> As the imagination far and near
> Travelled deep night. We'd see small companies,
>> Without exploit of cities, yoke the world one
> And among them, salvation clear, we'd see
>> In the white flame rejoicing for God's son
> Tysilio, who rather than draw his sword
>> Chose exile here, ceased to be Meifod's lord.[6]

The poem shows us a Baptist family in 1916 remembering a seventh-century Celtic saint at the coming of the New Year. In itself it tells us much of the tenaciousness and vitality of the Christian tradition in Wales, its capacity to cross the centuries, its capacity to cross the barriers caused by religious controversy and division. Waldo's father was the headmaster of the village school at Llandysilio, a keen and convinced Baptist. The family were active members of the nearby chapel at Blaen Comin. Waldo's parents were, moreover, Baptists of what would have been considered strongly progressive and radical views. They looked for the coming of God's kingdom here on earth, not only in the lives of individuals, but in the struggle for peace and righteousness in society, national and international. They were at this time strongly critical of the unthinking war fervour which had swept through Wales no less than England in the first years of the war. Already Waldo was a pacifist at heart, and the cause of pacifism was to become more and more central in his life, leading him to join the Society of Friends in 1953 and to go to prison in the early 1960s for refusing to pay his taxes to support the war in Korea and Cyprus.

But the church bell which is ringing in the New Year belongs to the parish church, at that time still a parish of the Church of England. The Church in Wales did not become an autonomous province in the Anglican Communion until 1919, and the struggle over the disestablishment of the church had been sharp and bitter in the previous decade. This is a parish belonging to an established church still identified in the minds of Welsh non-conformists with the alien power against which Waldo struggled throughout his life. But in the poem there is no hint of all this. The bell which is ringing is simply the bell of the village church, the church as the *hen fam*, the old mother, a term of surprising affection, still at times used in Welsh for the Church in Wales. It is simply the historic church of the place, the church of Tysilio from which the village takes its name. And to think of Tysilio, and the community which he drew together around him, is already to think of the wonder of the healing light which Christ's gospel can bring.

We do not know much of the life of Tysilio but much of what we know is referred to in the poem. He is a man whose story is anchored at Meifod, in Maldwyn/Montgomeryshire, the centre of the kingdom of Powys. He is a member of the princely house who renounces his royal rights in order to

follow the monastic way. This inevitably leads to conflict
with his family. Once, twice, perhaps more often, he spends
considerable periods away from mid Wales. He lived for a
time in Gwynedd on the island opposite to Bangor, Ynys
Tysilio. He lived for a time in the south, here on the borders
of Pembrokeshire and Carmarthenshire. E.G. Bowen suggests, 'The location of these outlying dedications strongly
suggests that St Tysilio did on some occasion journey along
the much frequented western sea-route so beloved by many
another Celtic saint'.[7] But always he retained links with
Meifod, and the scatter of churches dedicated to him in mid
Wales suggests land journeys as well.

We are not of course to suppose that all these thoughts
were present in any clear or articulate way in the mind of the
schoolboy who was Waldo. But as a general impression their
roots were there. What becomes explicit in the poem is the
result of a lifetime's study and reflection.

In his commentary on the poem Tony Conran sees three
times inseparably linked together. There is the present
moment in which we read it. There is the moment early in
this century when the incident took place. There is the time
so many hundred years ago when Tysilio lived and worked.
'As one reads the poem one suddenly sees that there are three
times involved, each with its own future implied. First . . .
there is the time of Tysilio's choice of exile rather than the
power of the sword, when the small companies of monks
yoked the world in one and salvation was like a clear flame.
Secondly there is the poet's own boyhood, on New Year's eve,
when the bells of the church rang in hope for a better year.
Thirdly there is now, the poet being amazed.'

Conran, in his discussion of the poem, underlines the
importance of the place itself in the whole complex of mem-
ories and thoughts. 'The poem is called Llandysilio-yn-
Nyfed, the parish, the village community gathered round

Tysilio's church; and about Waldo himself as a boy as part of that community. It remembers the experience of waiting outside for the New Year, of the bells ringing, of the family going indoors filled with wonder. Such ritual interruptions of the everyday are designed to release the imagination to make contact with what is important – in this case the Light that manifested Christ to Tysilio. On a purely empirical level that is what the poem is about. It is a picture of a community in action, at one of its moments of remembrance and hope, taking sustenance from the past to give to the future.'[8]

This surely is wonderfully well said and tells us much about the nature of tradition, and the way in which past and present are related. But the more I look at the poem the more I am also aware of the person of Tysilio himself and of Waldo's direct awareness of him. He sees Tysilio as a man at once rooted and journeying, uniting one place with another in those early centuries of Wales, when life was often brutal and quarrelsome. He is rooted in his commitment to Christ, a commitment expressed in his rejection of the sword and his creation of small non-violent communities of men and women dedicated to a life of prayer, penitence and praise. As the bell rang, the boy, already passionately interested in the history and meaning of his land, felt strangely at one with him. He thought of how Tysilio had gathered the different regions of Wales together into a single family; he thought of those early Christian communities, small companies without the 'exploit of cities'. Later he was to write, 'In me Wales is one'.

The word for exploit in Welsh is one which implies struggle, competition, success and achievement. The exploits of Tysilio's communities were of a different order from those of urban or industrial life. Their exploits were of a kind which speaks of compassion and co-operation, care and concern. These communities were certainly not without their own order and discipline. They *yoked* the world in one. And if this word reminds us of the saying of Jesus, 'My yoke is easy and my burden is light', it also suggests the story of St David, in whose monastery it is said the monks took the yoke from the oxen and ploughed the fields themselves. Gentleness and severity, kindness and toughness are not necessarily opposed to one another.

The vision of salvation in Christ needs to be tough as well as gentle, for it has to speak and become incarnate in a time when 'Life for us was brutal, full of wrong, Made great by neither purpose nor ideal'. These words speak directly of the early centuries of Britain after the collapse of the Roman Empire in the time of the Anglo-Saxon invasions. They speak directly of 1916 and 1917, the years of the Somme, and no less directly of 1996 as in Britain we begin to take stock of the dehumanising effects of more than fifteen years of Thatcherism.

The mixture of strength and gentleness which characterises Tysilio is to be seen in another very different poem which also dates from Waldo's later years. This is a hymn written to commemorate the centenary of the destruction of the church at Cwm yr Eglwys, on the north Pembrokeshire coast, by a great storm in 1859. It is dedicated to the person of St Brynach, an Irish saint, who founded the church there and who then established himself a few miles further on at Nevern (Nanhyfer). Those who know that place, the church-yard with its yew trees and its great standing cross situated at the heart of a typical Pembrokeshire valley, will know it as a place full of a sense of presence. A contemporary Welsh poet, who writes in English, says of it:

> Nevern, signed with David's cross and Brynach's,
> lay hushed and innocent. We stood
> in the sunny churchyard. Tower and trees

rippled with heat-haze, as if a tiny breeze,
passed over baptismal water
in golden font.[9]

Brynach's story like that of many Celtic saints is full alike
of angels and animals, as though people in those earlier centuries took for granted a confident access to areas of the
created world which for us are either non-existent or altogether inaccessible.

In his hymn, however, Waldo speaks not of these stories
but of the basic fact of the restoration of kinship between
earth and heaven to which the life of the saint bears witness.
This he believes to be as true for us now as it was then, not
least through the interweaving of Brynach's prayers with ours.
The lines are those of a hymn for congregational singing.
They have a directness and formality not typical of Waldo's
more lyrical and personal statements.

> Lord, shepherd of the ages of the earth,
> > Awakener of the grey mornings of our land,
> Your saints stand in glory,
> > Over and around the places where we dwell.
> You have given to us on the wasteland of time
> > The light of an immortal hour,
> You have rekindled in our spirit
> > The ancient kinship of earth and heaven.

The poet goes on to pray that God will cleanse our hearts and
strengthen our arms; that through the hidden veins of the
earth the living water of the holy wells and springs of Wales
may come to refresh us; that we may find at those wells, as did
the woman at Jacob's well in Samaria, that we are face to
face with the king of glory. Here, as in other places, Waldo
combines biblical motifs with motifs taken from the world of

nature and of Welsh tradition. For him, as for Islwyn in the nineteenth century, the story of the meeting at Jacob's well in Samaria at once leads to thoughts of the innumerable holy wells of Wales.

> You gave Brynach to us as a guardian,
>   He raised the cross above the waves,
> The storm of love on Golgotha
>   Established peace in his heart;
> Brynach, Irishman, look on us,
>   Let our prayers flow together with yours
> So that the strong walls may be raised
>   Above the tempests of this world's sea.[10]

The confidence that the hymn expresses in the sharing of prayer across the barriers of death is particularly striking in this verse when we remember that the writer was a Quaker of non-conformist origins who had previously been a Baptist. There is here a coming together of Catholic and Evangelical convictions which creates something new, which is also the rediscovery of something very old, confidence in the communion of saints, in the power of God to bind us in one, across the barriers of time and death.

II

The living sense of tradition which we find in Waldo Williams can be found also in the other poets of this period. Their understanding of tradition involves both horizontal and vertical dimensions. The horizontal implies a careful handing on through history of a precious and carefully cultivated heritage. The vertical implies at the same time the possibility of an unexpected and unpredictable new creation; the original may suddenly reassert itself. God the Holy Spirit who breathes where he will can make new again what has become old. The tradition can come to new life at any moment, but for this to happen, it must, at least in principle, be there. There must be its tenacious passing on from one generation to another.

This double nature of tradition can be seen in an outstanding poem of Waldo's contemporary, Gwenallt. It is a poem which takes us to one of the great historic centres of early Welsh Christianity, Llanbadarn Fawr, and shows us a celebration of the eucharist taking place. The sacrament links past and present in a continuous history, but at the same time it opens the world of time to the coming of the eternal world and to the pentecostal power of the Spirit. In the Word and the Spirit eternity breaks into our darkened fear-filled world. The poem is striking in giving us another example of the way in which the world is seen as sacramental, and the celebration of the church's eucharist is seen as having consequences not only for the whole of society but also for the whole of nature.

Gwenallt begins with images which convey a sense of imperfection, anxiety and guilt. The world is somehow unclean and we feel ourselves to be unclean in it. This too is a time which is brutal and full of wrong. The church building at Llanbadarn, which is in fact unusually large for a Welsh parish church, conveys a sense of strangeness and awe. There is nothing of the feeling of the nearness and intimacy of God which the little village churches of Wales can convey.

> There was disease in the air and things had an unhealthy
>   look to them,
> All nature's colours were edged with an inky stain,
> A shepherd on the hillside gathered his sheep and
>   counted them,
> Counted the sheep stupid with sins, rotten and worm
>   eaten.

It was quiet in the church, and in the quietness fear,
Fear of the altar and the cross, and the east end with its
    glass
And the chancel so far and strange, the roof over its
    head so high,
And we down on the ground kneeling like dark and
    dirty clods.

It is into this diseased and uneasy world that the mercy and
glory of God descend. The sacrament is the presence of the
incarnate Christ here and now, in the midst of a life which is
full of imperfection and disarray.

Bethlehem came down from heaven into the middle of
    the communion service,
With its angels and shepherds and its mute unsatisfied
    animals,
And Mary tidily folding up God's immortality in his
    nappy,
And rocking eternity to sleep in his cradle.

Christ has come to be one with us, sharing the finitude and
limitations of our world. He has come to be one with us in
order to lift us up into the openness and immensity of his
kingdom. His birth at Bethlehem carries hidden within itself
the death which overcomes death, as we see in the Eastern
icons of the nativity which show the swaddled infant placed
in a dark cave, reminding us of the bound body of the cruci-
fied master placed in the dark cave of the tomb.

He did not fling out our bit of flesh like a rag onto the
    rubbish dump of Gehenna,
Or throw out our blood there like a bottle of used up
    medicine,

101

But he raised them from the grip of the worm's unparalleled three days
As a translucent spiritual body, the perfection of man
and God.

There follows what is in some ways the most perplexing
verse in the poem. After these direct theological affirmations
there comes a reference to a sound of running water in the
chancel, a little stream of devotion reminding us of a fountain
in the square of a southern city. This image is at once followed by another; a ray of sunlight from outside the church
obliterating the feeble light of the candles on the altar, a
direct revelation of the humanity of God. It is this verse
which I take to refer most clearly to the dual nature of the
church's tradition, an eternal reality constantly recreated by
the newness of the Spirit's action, so that every eucharist is at
once a little Pentecost and at the same time an historical
event with its stubbornly maintained links which take us back
through time as well as space. Here we are led back from our
dark northern landscape to the brilliant light of the Mediterranean cities in which the first Christian communities
developed and grew.

There was a sound of trickling water in the chancel, as in
the square of an Italian city,
A little stream along the bed of custom and devotion
from the wells of heaven
And a ray of sunlight playing around the cross and obliterating the light of the candles,
A spark from the bonfire of his divine humanity.

In the final verse the two elements of fire and water which
have already been present in the lines just quoted suddenly
invade the picture with apocalyptic power.

And outside the mortal darkness of the yew tree in
  Llanbadarn
Became a green spring bursting all over into song,
And the sea galloped in to embrace Rheidol and
  Ystwyth,
And its crests were aflame and all its waves were on
  fire.[11]

The transfiguration of the whole creation in the light of the
sacrament of Christ's divine humanity is affirmed with a
directness and a vigour typical of Gwenallt. In the eucharist,
birth, death, resurrection and the coming of the pentecostal
Spirit, all become present, and in that presence all things
are transformed. Again the poem speaks of continuities in
discontinuities in time, of an eternal reality made known here
and now.

This work appeared in Gwenallt's last collection of verse,
Y Coed, which was published posthumously in 1969. In the
latter years of his life Gwenallt had returned to the Calvinistic Methodism in which he had grown up, having felt
more and more alienated by the Englishness of the Church in
Wales as he found it at that time. But this return to his roots
did not involve the repudiation of the insights which he had
gained in his Anglican days. The poem speaks out of a
powerfully Catholic sacramental faith, and its vision of Llanbadarn as a place of historic connectedness as well as of
pentecostal renewal speaks of a balance and fullness of theological understanding which may well draw our admiration.

III

We have been looking at the work of poets who first made
their name in the middle years of this century and we have
also been thinking of the way in which the development of

the Welsh tradition is full of surprises. This has remained true in the years which have followed since that time. In the subsequent decades there have been two new developments in particular in Welsh poetry, both of which would need much greater space than can be given here for any adequate appreciation of them, both of which it would have been difficult to foresee.

The first is the revival of writing in the 'strict-metres', a movement which has taken Welsh writers and readers of poetry back into the roots of the poetic method and technique that flourished in the middle ages. In recent years this movement has revealed an amazing capacity to release new life and vision and it has drawn in people from a great variety of backgrounds and experience. Since the founding of the periodical *Barddas* in 1976, and the subsequent growth of the publishing house of the same name, the movement has been particularly identified with Alan Llwyd, perhaps the best-known poet in Welsh-speaking Wales today, a man of immense energy and dedication, a poet of great and original genius. Needless to say, work written in this school has often been deeply marked by the Christian elements in the Welsh poetic tradition which we have been studying, and much remains to be written about it.

The second new movement in Welsh poetry is, if anything, more recent, and while it parallels developments in other languages and cultures it is perhaps particularly significant in a Welsh context. With the two solitary exceptions of Ann Griffiths in the eighteenth century and Gwerfyl Mechain in the fifteenth, the Welsh poetic tradition has been overwhelmingly masculine. Suddenly, in the last twenty-five years, a whole series of women poets have begun to make their voices heard, Nesta Wyn Jones (1946–), Menna Elfyn (1951–), Einir Jones (1950–), Gwyneth Lewis (1959–), to mention only a few representative names.

Of course it is not only in our Western European, North American world that the voices of women are heard in new ways. All over the world things which have not been said before, or at least have not been said aloud and in print, are finding new expression. We are led to see the world in new perspectives. Our whole consciousness of what it is to be human shifts and changes, in ways which are disconcerting but also full of promise and new insight.

Amongst the writers who have been named, one in particular demands our attention. Not only does Gwyneth Lewis write from a thoroughly feminine point of view, she writes with great fluency both in Welsh and in English, in a way which has few, if any, precedents. 'Linguistically my domestic arrangements are unusual for a poet. I live in a literary ménage à trois, but the muse is kind and I get to write poems in both languages. Both Welsh and English are so delightful, how could I ever choose between them? When in trouble I pray in Welsh, I want Welsh psalms read to me on my death bed. I swear and count in English, and am still learning new words at the fringes of the well planted English forest. . . .'[12]

One of the finest of her English poems begins:

> Lord of the Running Rivers
> I was given two languages
> to speak, or rather they have spoken me
> through different landscapes from a common spring.[13]

Whether such a wholly bilingual poetic gift can be maintained for more than one lifetime, or whether it is something made possible by the present moment in the relationship of the two languages is difficult to say. What is evident is that the gift is here, and we need to rejoice in it.

One would think it would be necessarily the case that after the overwhelmingly male character of the poetic tradition in

Wales, the transition to another mode would involve some degree of protest, an element of violence. One can see that in some places in the writings of the women poets of Wales. What seems to me more striking is the element of continuity through change which is also evident. Old themes appear in new guises.

There is, for instance, a poem of Menna Elfyn, 'Power Cut', which gives a wonderful account of the results of a power failure for a shared meal. Candles are lit, a kettle is boiled on the hob, the rate of things slows down and we can enjoy one another's company, the social content of the meal is newly realised.

> And the ceremony
> unwittingly becomes our celebration
> of family across the table.[14]

But it is in a sequence of poems by Gwyneth Lewis, written originally in Welsh and translated into English by the poet, that we see most striking signs of continuity with themes which we have been considering in this chapter. The sequence is called *Wholeness*, and it reflects on the way in which human beings are called to unite in themselves two worlds, an evident everyday world, a more hidden secret world in 'the room beyond the weather'.

One of these poems, 'Llanbadarn Baptism 1843', provides a wonderful and quite unconscious foil to Gwenallt's poem about the eucharist at Llanbadarn. Here, no less than in the earlier poem, time and eternity, Wales and Palestine coincide. But here the sacrament is celebrated out of doors, and the whole occasion has a festive and delightfully feminine aspect.

> The day they baptised
> Margaret Ann

the Jordan
flowed through Llanbadarn.

Margaret Ann goes down into the water, feels

The water's weight
its turbulent history,

experiencing in her own way the waters of the flood. But the
mood is one of celebration.

Her sister waved her parasol;
the saints stood like flowers
along the banks
of the crystal Rheidol
while along it, the lions
of Providence
roared out their blessings
to Aberystwyth
while she and the minister,
they both wore
the river like stockings
in hosanna style
while watching two worlds –
one rural, parochial,
the other divine –
both flowing together
while the Sunday hats
were ready for Judgement
and she, the bride,
our Margaret Ann
was dazzling
lovely, fully at one
with the brilliant sun

which blessed and protected
the sighing palms
that had sprung up
in fertile Llanbadarn.[15]

In the final poem of the sequence, called simply 'The Icon',
the writer gives an extremely perceptive account of what is
involved in sanctity, the life of God shining out through a
human face. In classical Welsh and Irish poetry the first and
last verses of a poem often correspond, following a spiral
route which brings us back to the place where we started
but further on. Here the first verse gives us an immediate
impression of an icon; this isn't a man at all but a cast of soul.
But the last verse takes us much further; the cast of soul is
truly embodied in the human person who knows and suffers
all in full.

This isn't a man but a cast of soul
one who, rewarded for seeing in part,
was given the talent of being whole.

His body shows his disposition:
how questions are stairs to a greater faith,
how patience in him is a pattern . . .

He has died into the energy
which makes him nothing, but gives him all
life in his serenity.

His body is an opening door
as he feels the presence of his Lord,
giver of all that's enough and more,

who speaks in the grammar of broken saints

whose pain is sweetest music, for
their dying nerves fulfil love's law.

His eyes are far away as the moon,
his mouth a flower without spittle's dew
the world a desert to a man who, soon,

transformed and quickened, shall quench his thirst
in streams of uncreated light
which judge the best and love the worst

for he is a man with a cast of soul
who dared to abandon his seeing in part
for knowing, for suffering all in full.[16]

If Waldo Williams' poems can remind us of icons, here, forty years later, we have a writer who is familiar with the classical icon of the Christian East and also with some of its distinctive theology. She reads in the icons many of the salient characteristics of Christian holiness. The saint himself can become an icon, a window, a door through which the wholeness of God may come, healing and pacifying.

Tradition is not, as is often thought, something static or wholly of the past. The word 'tradition' itself implies the handing on of life and that means the capacity to change and grow and to be open to the future. The astonishing fruitfulness of the Welsh literary tradition in this century, its capacity to become new both by exploring new areas and by rediscovering old and forgotten ones, is a sign of its vitality. It is also a sign that poetry, being on the side of life, can bear witness, in ever new ways, to the deity's immemorial attribute of infinite personal concern. The witness that it bears for the most part is indirect and implicit, but it is nonetheless real on that account.

CHAPTER SIX

There Is No Resurrection Where There Is No Earth:

Euros Bowen and Bobi Jones

We have said at the beginning of this study that God's presence makes the world. Through the active presence of the Word by whom all things were made and in whom God's wisdom is at work the world is endowed with coherence and direction. Through the active presence of the Spirit who is Lord and creator of life, the whole creation is filled with vitality, grows and develops in an immense variety of ways.

This God who creates is at the same time the God three-in-one, revealed in Jesus Christ, made known in the coming of the Spirit at Pentecost. In such a vision of things there is no separation, above all no opposition, between the revelation of God in redemption, in the history of salvation which centres in the person of Jesus, and the revelation of God in creation, in the evolution of all things, including at their heart the whole history of the human family.

This is a way of seeing things, in which the book of the world illumines the book of the scriptures, and in which the book of the scriptures illumines the world. It is, as we have seen, to be found in the earliest Welsh religious poetry of which we have a record. This interweaving of the work of creation with the work of redemption continues to be present in a great variety of ways, some more explicit, others less, throughout the centuries of the Welsh tradition.

One particular expression of it is to be found in the poetry of Euros Bowen (1904–1988), one of the outstanding poets of the second half of this century. The theological quality of his work is not altogether surprising. Euros was not only a poet but also a scholar and a priest. As a young man he had thought of becoming a theological teacher and had dreamt of writing a definitive study of Karl Barth in Welsh. He had a good grasp of the classics; his knowledge of Greek and Latin was extensive, and while he is remembered for his translations of Virgil and Sophocles, it is important to note that he also translated Athanasius' *On the Incarnation* into Welsh.

The style and method of his poetry was often called symbolist, partly because he had been influenced by the French writers of that school, but more because he believed that the primary material of poetry is to be found in symbols and images, rather than in ideas and concepts. He himself however always insisted that his poetic method was not symbolist but sacramental. To him this distinction was of vital importance. The method of his poetry was in accordance with its content, and this, as he constantly said, was to praise and celebrate the 'sacramental elements of the goodness', present throughout the universe.[1] One of his volumes was called simply *Elfennau/Elements* and he was particularly pleased with the design on the dust jacket which showed a series of small circles discreetly suggesting the wafers used in the sacrament of communion.

We noted in our first chapter that a view of the inter-relationship of God's revelation of himself in creation with his revelation of himself in redemption is in no way the possession of the Celtic Christian tradition alone. It is clearly formulated in one of the greatest and most representative

111

teachers of the Christian East. For the Orthodox Church there is no separation between these two ways. In both God is at work. 'That is why St Maximus the Confessor does not posit an essential distinction between natural revelation and the supernatural or biblical one. According to him the latter is only the embodying of the former in historical persons and actions.' In the events of the history of salvation, above all in the mystery of Christ's death and resurrection, the innermost meaning and direction of the whole of creation is revealed and confirmed.

On account of the fall, that is to say our alienation from God and our own true selves, our minds are often darkened and our wills baffled and confused. The saving revelation of Christ makes clear and gives wholly new strength to the deep and universal, but in many ways uncertain, perceptions of general revelation. As Maximus maintains, 'supernatural revelation merely restores direction to, and provides a more determined support for that inner movement maintained within the world by God through natural revelation'. These sentences with their summary of the thought of Maximus come from the opening pages of Dumitru Staniloae's *Dogmatic Theology*, one of the outstanding twentieth-century Orthodox presentations of the Christian faith. They are fundamental for Staniloae's own understanding of his subject.[2]

No less striking on this point is the conclusion of Lars Thunberg at the end of his masterly study of Maximus' understanding of human nature and human persons. 'Nature and grace are not in opposition to each other, for when human nature is truly developed, it is open to divine grace which establishes that relation to God for which human nature was created.'[3]

This means that without the discovery of the general revelation latent in the substance of things, in the most everyday events, the special revelation of God's love in Christ loses its meaning, its rootedness in the lived experience of women and men. It is only as it is realised in flesh and blood that we begin to discover the true capacity of the gospel to redeem, heal and transform the dark and deeply wounded areas of human life and experience. Taken on its own, without this deep relationship with the world, 'Religion' becomes something on its own, a small department of life cut off from the common joys and sorrows of humanity. As Euros Bowen declares, 'There is no resurrection where there is no earth. *Nid oes atgyfodiad lle nad oes pridd.*'[4]

Seen in such a light the poetry of Euros Bowen can be recognised as theological through and through. To many of those who have read him this affirmation might seem a misunderstanding. On the surface there is far less about what we call Christianity in his writing than there is in the poetry of his contemporaries Gwenallt or Waldo Williams. He is a poet who seems only seldom to speak about religious things, about the events of the gospel or the faith of the church. Of course there are glancing references to such things in his work but they are usually discreet. This is not by chance, for Euros wanted his writing to celebrate and proclaim the hidden anonymous activities of God, 'the sacramental elements of the goodness' which are so deeply buried in things as to be often unperceived.

I

A very clear example of this can be seen in a poem called simply '*Tendency*', which takes the form of a conversation between two voices, one which constantly questions, the other which responds. It was a commissioned poem, written to be recorded and used in the 'Dial-a-poem' service which the Welsh Arts Council sponsored for a time in the seventies.

113

Darkness tends towards light.

Just how?

Like a window in the night
    edging towards the moon
a skylark climbing
    to the rafters of the sky
the song of a thrush
    on the mast of trees.

In what way?

Like the tempo of the wind
    along the forest fence
mice peering out of the cellars of the stars
the owl's eyes cursing

    a car's headlights
a flute pouring out
    along the bottom of the valley.

And its appearance?

Like waves where rocks ascend,
the sound of a bell in lighthouse mist
mushrooms under an August haze
the silence of leaves
    in September frost.

And its form?

Like drawing the curtains in a hospital ward
the perfume of roses

> along a garden path
> snow thawing with the shudder
> of coarse grass on the frith.
>
> In what manner?
>
> Like a cloudless thirst
> along a merciless strip of land
> and its hunger spreading
> like flood waters.
>
> And what kind of sight?
>
> – a grey sea when it begins to whiten
> and the blackness of the earth rising green.[5]

What we have here are six answers to a series of brief questions, all collected under the affirmation with which the poem starts: 'Darkness tends towards light'. This is the nearest thing that we have in the poem to a specifically theological or religious statement. Indeed we might say that the theological point of the poem as a whole is precisely that there are no theological references in it. Each of the six replies points to places, times or situations in which points of light, or suggestions of new life, are observed in situations of apparent darkness, discouragement and despair. There is the window edging towards the moon, the curtains pulled back in the hospital ward. There are the eyes of the mice peering out, small creatures that can see in the dark, their eyes points of light in a place of gloom. There is the seeming rebuke of the eyes of wild creatures caught in the stabbing rays of our headlights. Here we may feel the poet projects into the reactions of the owl something of his own feelings in meeting oncoming headlights undipped.

115

Immediately afterwards we pass to a wholly different image of refreshment and relief. The sound of a flute 'pouring out along the bottom of the valley'. In Welsh the word for pouring, *tywalltiad*, itself suggests the sound of water being poured. In the penultimate answer which speaks of a cloudless thirst and a spreading hunger, we begin to feel the force and urgency of this tendency, this movement, this thrust from darkness towards light. It is no small power which we are involved with here; it is the power which will give birth to a new creation. It is the power of a grey sea turning to whiteness, the power which brings the black of earth up into a living green. When he recited this poem the poet would pronounce these last words with great and rising emphasis.

The same point is made a little more explicitly in a better-known poem called 'This is Praise'. This poem has a certain notoriety in Welsh because it involves a direct response to one of the great poets of the first half of the century, R. Williams Parry. Williams Parry ends one of his sonnets with the words, 'Death does not die; this is woe.' Euros' conclusion is simply, 'Life does not die, this is praise.'

When we come to examine the poem, however, we find as so often in his work that the images are predominantly natural, images which suggest the turning of the seasons, the return of life after winter, or the renewal of life in a community as generation succeeds to generation.

> And when the swallow,
> its diligent nesting done,
> has left for the south,
> I have seen summer decay
> as an acorn rolls golden
> into the shadow of the country's oak.

But none of these images will of themselves take us further

than the round of life and death which we observe in the world of nature. Is there no more to be said? There is, for in the lines which follow we hear of

> the smile of the departed
> before burial in the earth.[6]

It is these two lines which lead directly to the poem's final affirmation. Here there is clearly, though still only implicitly, an appeal to faith in the resurrection of Christ. It was a point where the poet spoke out of a moment of deep significance for himself. For, as he once confided, it reflected his own experience in seeing the serene happiness which seemed to mark his father's face at the moment of death.

As one becomes more accustomed to the manner of Euros' poetry, so one becomes more alert to the theological directions hidden in it. A very striking example of this is to be seen in a brief poem called 'A Red Poppy'. The significance of poppies in November – Euros was fourteen at the end of the First World War – alerts us to the theme of sacrifice, but it hardly prepares us for all that the poem suggests about the gift of the Spirit, the gift of life won through the agony of death.

> Is that a religion of comfort.
> when the sower,
> in picking up stones
> and weeding the thorns and the briars,
> has to bleed
> for his pains?
>
> But on the breeze
> his wounds released
> a poem

from the hillock of the headland,
like a red poppy in the corn,
and called it another comforter.[7]

In a note to his long poem 'Genesis', Euros speaks of a
poem as 'a pattern of images and meaning', and he adds 'an
image, as I see it, makes the *meaning* of which it is a sign real
to us; it makes the reality of the meaning present'. The
images in 'A Red Poppy' surely act in this way. The sower is
wounded in the sowing; the spirit-breeze makes from the
wounds a source of comfort. The images bring meanings
before us and make them present in a many-levelled way
which simple concepts fail to do.

Euros had a fear lest the church, in our century, should
turn the gospel into a mere set of words and concepts, an
ideology, which it could package and communicate at will.
The communication of the mystery of God's love was for him
not only a matter of words but also of significant signs and
actions. In a poem called 'The Word', which is in fact about
the sacrament of holy communion, he says that in celebrating
that rite God himself comes to us

as confidence for men . . .
with the light which breaks forth from the mystery
so that the word of grace shall not be an ideology of
   Christ.[8]

II

This use of imagery with a sacramental purpose can be seen
at its most developed in the long poem 'Genesis' which was
entered as the 'chair' poem at the National Eisteddfod in
Llandudno in 1963. The subject of the poem was given;

Euros chose to treat it by way of the impression made on him by the baptistry window in the newly opened cathedral at Coventry. The window, which takes the form of a great sunburst, is one of John Piper's most successful creations. It moved Euros deeply; he saw in its glory and its colours an image of the uncreated light of God dividing itself out into the many colours of creation.

His poem is divided into three parts. The first speaks of the creation of the world and human kind, the second the incarnation and the birth of the Son of God, and the third, which is much shorter, of the birth of the Christian through water and the Spirit. The content of the poem is classical and so is the form. Euros takes one of the most difficult verse forms from medieval Welsh and uses it with superb assurance. The whole of the first section of the poem, eighty lines in all, uses a single rhyme.[9]

The judges were divided in their assessment of the poem. Only one of them, Tom Parry, thought it deserved the 'chair'. His two colleagues found it wilfully and unnecessarily obscure. The poem certainly is difficult, but it is not a difficulty which should have defeated a man of the intellectual calibre of T.H. Parry-Williams, who was the second judge. It is difficult not to feel that his distaste for the poem was caused, perhaps unconsciously, by its uncompromising Christian orthodoxy and above all by the fact that the central section dwells at length on the figure of Mary.[10]

The key word in the poem, as Tom Parry clearly saw, is *berw*, a word which Euros translates as 'creative ferment – the thrill of the creative imagination: the *berw* in and through the pattern of images and meaning'. H.A. Hodges, who made a translation of the poem into English remarks, 'the subject of the ode is not the window, but genesis as signified in the window. But the two cannot be kept apart. The ferment of colours in the church becomes a ferment of ideas in the poet's

119

mind and in this again he sees the ferment of the divine activity'.

'Genesis', is a poem which deserves more attention than it has received. It is one of the many remarkable works which the newly built Coventry Cathedral inspired. The images which it uses are taken sometimes from scripture, sometimes from Christian tradition, sometimes specifically from the land of Wales. In one of his notes on the poem Bowen writes of a passage in the second section, 'in the orchard, in the vineyard, in the church (*yn y berllan, yn y winllan, yn y llan*) the Virgin is a cup, a grail for the blood of the Spirit, wedded to the praise of the Holy Spirit'.

The ferment of new birth which the poem describes with such abundance of natural imagery itself proceeds from the desire, the longing of the creator. The word for desire in the original is *awydd*, a word which conveys something of the meaning of *eros* in Greek, the divine *eros* or desire of which Dionysius speaks so powerfully, which draws God out from himself into the agony of his creation. Euros himself commented, 'I think of man as endowed on the finite level with creative freedom, God as creative freedom on the infinite level. *Awydd* implies the exercise of freedom.'

If we look for a moment at the third and slightest part of the poem, the section which speaks of baptism as birth through water and the Spirit, it is interesting to note that Euros speaks of both water and oil, of baptism and chrismation.

> Water from shining hillside stream,
> Earth, grove, after last year's snow,
> True water that is oil of mercy to many,
> Water of begetting, making an heir.

These are images which have much in common with those of

120

Tudur Aled in his poem in praise of the waters of St Wini-
fred's Well.

> The water of baptism is the fresh growth of the world
> And is called the font of the healing oil of faith.[11]

Once again the sacraments are seen in relation not just to the
church and to humanity but to the whole world of nature.

So we have here a work of the imagination which is at once
highly traditional in its basic form and content, yet highly
original in its use of imagery, a new work of poetic art called
out by a new work of visual art. Seen against the background
of the history we have been examining in these pages we can
see how true it is to the tradition of theological poetry which
was inaugurated in the first millennium. In its clear trinitarian structure and in its emphasis on the place of Mary, in its
holding together of the different dimensions of Christian
faith, personal and universal, creative and redemptive, we can
see characteristics which link it with the earliest examples of
religious verse in Welsh.

In the last decades of his life, after his retirement, Euros
increasingly enjoyed holidays in the world around the eastern
Mediterranean, Israel and Jordan, Turkey, Cyprus and
Greece. In them his love for the classical world and his love
for the world of the Bible both found expression. Like Gwenallt, at the end of his life, he found himself more and more
drawn to Eastern Orthodoxy. He was fascinated by icons, by
the great mosaic Pantocrator in the cathedral at Cefalu and
by an icon of the last supper by Michael Damascinos in a
church in Herakleion, an icon which attempts to fuse
elements of Renaissance painting with the Byzantine tradition.

Above all he was captured by the fresco of the resurrection
which he found in the side chapel of the Church of Our

Saviour in Chora in Istanbul. The figure of Christ, pulling up Adam and Eve, the representatives of all humanity, out of the place of death, into the land of the living, spoke to him powerfully. The church, when he visited it, was in a run-down, semi-suburban area far from the centre of the city. It was a place without much shape or form to it, 'a shabby enough place'. But all is transformed by the unlooked for glory within which fulfils the promise of the words with which the poem opens, words which are placed at the entrance to the church and give the church its name.

> *He Chora Ton Zonton,* – the Land of the Living,
> those were the words,
> in a shabby enough place,
> on the mosaic of the old Byzantine church
> on the outskirts of the city of Istanbul,
>
> and the city an old garden
> became a withered land,
> an old pleasure became a graveyard,
> an old sanctuary a museum,
>
> if it wasn't for the stirring of a fresco
> a Resurrection,
> the hands of its glory
> reaching out for
> and drawing the wonder
> of Adam and Eve
> up
> out of their graves,
> in a shabby enough place,
> into the land of the living.[12]

122

III

As we have seen in the work of Euros Bowen, one of the great advantages of the poetic use of images is that it makes it possible to present both the universality and the particularity of God's presence in the world. The image can at one and the same time encompass the particular and the universal. This, which is true of Euros Bowen's poetry, is also true of the work of Bobi Jones. Born in 1929 Bobi Jones belongs to a younger generation than the three poets whose work we have been considering. He grew up in Cardiff in a thoroughly anglicised environment. Only during his secondary schooling did he begin to learn Welsh. These facts make his literary productivity all the more remarkable.

Bobi Jones is without doubt one of the most prolific and active of all Welsh writers in the twentieth century, a poet, a novelist and a scholar who has written in the fields of literary criticism and literary theory, of education and educational psychology, theology and spirituality. In giving an account of his poetic work, it is difficult to know where to begin. But I believe this stress on the particular as opposed to the abstract is one of the keys to understanding it and I intend to follow this line by looking at the way in which, in his work, the frozen sameness of evil and death is constantly contrasted with the luxuriant variety of life and goodness.

Bobi Jones is the only contemporary Welsh poet who has had a substantial body of his poetry published in English translation. This work has been done by Joseph Clancy, an American scholar now very actively retired in Wales, who rivals Tony Conran in his work as a translator of Welsh. Clancy indeed has worked both in prose and poetry, translating, for instance, Kate Roberts' short stories and Saunders Lewis' plays. He too is a man who speaks from inside the poetic process, being himself a poet as well as a translator, and a theologian as well as a poet.

In the introduction to his volume of translations, *Selected Poems*, Clancy writes of the capacity of the poet to hold together in his poetry the different aspects of his life and work in a richly differentiated unity. He quotes Henry James as saying 'It is a complex fate' to be an American. The same complexity seems to be there in the fate of the contemporary Welshman. The question of national identity can never be ignored.

The national strand in Bobi Jones' work is, he maintains, central and inescapable and yet it cannot be taken alone. 'Nationalism is not a . . . separable element in Bobi Jones' work – any more than are the other central experiences separable elements; love of the natural world, of wife, of children, of neighbour, of God through Christ, these are expressed as a unity within single poems as in the total body of his work.'[13]

Clancy goes on to point to that foundation of faith which enables this poet, like the other writers whose work we have been examining, to affirm the meaning of the life of things despite all the threats of vacuity and death. 'The ground of that unity is that experience of faith in Christ, in the incarnation and redemption, as a continuing divinely-given validation of the particular – this time, this place, this person, this event, this history, this language, this nation – as essential to human meaning and destiny, as a means of revelation, of grace.' This is precisely how we find Bobi Jones' poems in fact to be, affirmations of the transcendent value of the particular as essential to human meaning and destiny, a means of revelation and grace.

This affirmation of the particular necessarily involves a special stress on the diversity, the unexpectedness of things. Interestingly Bobi Jones sees this diversity as rooted in the resurrection. His thought here seems very close to that of some of the earliest Welsh and Irish writers who think of the resurrection of the body of Christ as involving the resurrection of all creation. Furthermore, resurrection means life, and life means diversity. Bobi Jones sees this in terms of the contrast between the frozen cold of evil and death, static and uniform, and the overflowing diversity of things that are alive; the sameness of cold and the abundance of love, in Welsh, *yn lle'r un oer – amlder cariad*.

We can see this in one of his best-known early poems called 'Spring at Nant Dywelan'. There can be no doubt about the specificity of the place, the two opening lines give us a clue to the whole poem.[14]

> I entered it before I understood it
> Knew it before I knew about it.

To know *about* the world is to know it simply as a problem we can solve or as a material we can master. But this is only a limited way of knowing, a way which is useful and necessary up to a point but which can become destructive and death-dealing when our desire to master and exploit the world we live in gets out of hand. We see this very clearly in the dangers which confront our living environment.

To know the world as the poet, or as the person who prays, knows it is to know it primarily as a mystery into which we enter; a mystery which is not closed but open to us and which summons us to ever deeper knowledge and understanding. In this perspective the world itself and every place within the world is seen not as a problem to be mastered and explained away but as a reality greater than ourselves to be progressively explored and known, loved and praised. To find the world in this way is to find it open towards eternity, open towards God. It is to find God present in it, speaking to us, giving himself to us.

Like smoke
The light ingathered round me
Head over heels through the leaves and the birds and the
  pasture
Like an unblemished lamb
In the primal freedom we sprang from,
And oh, I too leapt on the scent
Of vigour astir in the grass,
Of life and liveliness in the new-born brook.

The coming of spring is seen not only as the renewal of life; it is a conversion, a turning from death to life; it is the conquest of death. It is a stupendous energy which splits the world in two, opening up all the graves.

The year has known conversion.
It has; energy is everywhere. It splits the world.
It is the boundless Mystery that comforts being.
Down on the bank of the river the toads
And the water-vole bestir themselves
Beyond good and evil – I clear out of the way! –
Spreading their tender feet on the carcass of winter.

The words of the hymn sung over and over again in the Easter night service of the Orthodox Church come insistently to mind.

Christ is risen from the dead,
Trampling down death by death
And to those in the tombs giving life.

The cross is seen here, as in the Christianity of the first millennium, as the tree of life, the cross of victory. Death was

126

not overcome without a mortal combat, but it was indeed overcome.

> Winter has gone to its fathers.
> It was sharp; alive. And look at them here:
> Life has triumphed over life, and death death
> On this everlasting meadow that is
> A Cross for the year.
> Spring came through the mouth of the morning
> Its tongue clamouring hotly on the petals of sunrise
> Like the boots of a soldier coming home.

In the sound of the boots we hear the sound of the death which tramples down death.

If this poem gives us a picture of the vitality of spring, the power of cold to paralyse and kill is expressed in a series of verses which date from the year Bobi Jones spent teaching in the university in Quebec. The depth of the Canadian winter brought to his mind some of the 'gnomic' or proverbial verses to be found in early Welsh writing, which may well date from the tenth century or before. In them, as here, the poet, by constant repetition, gradually establishes his meaning.

> Coldness in land and in head
> Grass and leaves in absence:
> The snow is so tidy.

The coldness is inner and outer. The abundance and variety of living things is absent. There is a menacing tidiness about the snow.

> Coldness through root and through town:
> Heaven's cloud-pigs drive
> Prodigals homewards.

The coldness is felt in the natural and in the social world. The heavy snow clouds drive us home. Like the prodigal son we are faced with famine in a land which has become alien.

> Coldness on heart and hill:
> Ducks are not on the lake –
> Waters don't ask for them.

The freeze is in the heart as well as on the hill. Nature is seen in terms of responsive relationships which are also paralysed. The frozen waters don't welcome the ducks.

> Coldness through lip and house
> Even wind shivers
> So black is whiteness.

The wind itself feels the cold. The whiteness turns black.

> Coldness killing word in mouth,
> Comfort's not shared between two:
> The tradition's shut-down.

The coldness is explicitly death-dealing. It kills the living word; the word which links one to another and is itself a place of meeting. There is no longer strength or encouragement in human contact. The whole handing on of life breaks down.

> Coldness fluent along the sea bed
> Putting ice on my door-knob
> So it can never open.[15]

The cold penetrates to the depths of the sea. My door-knob freezes up. There is no more opening of the way ever again.
Against these icy verses we can place another poem from

128

later in the same sequence, 'The Resurrection of The Birds'. This is a poem which owes much to Dafydd ap Gwilym, not only because it uses the *cywydd* metre which he pioneered, but also because it follows a typical Dafydd strategy in its use of imagery. Dafydd tends to use, in a poem of this kind, two sets of images which run concurrently, sometimes clashing, sometimes interchanging. Here we have two sets of spring-time images, those which relate to water, those which relate to bird song. The thaw has come, water drips from roofs and eaves, the birds again are heard, singing, but perhaps even more, chirping. It is the chirping of the birds which is responsible for the drops of sound in which the poet bathes.

The poem ends with an extended use of the contrast between cold's sameness and love's abundance. The population explosion of the birds causes anxiety for the local government officials. They are a nightmare to neat order. They are altogether superfluous. What can we do with so much joy? How can we fit all these living gifts into the strait-jacket of the free-market economy?

> No land can be without birds.
> At least, no civilised land.
> Define the way one wishes:
> No eye is made without stars,
> True bard without lake water,
> Nor a roof without its bird.
>
> The roof thaws as melodies
> Now. The meadow musicians
> Are sprinkling a kilderkin
> Of drops of sound to cleanse me.
> I am open-mouthed beneath them
> Like fishes gulping the wind,
> Or chick in a nest waggling

Its beak as it welcomes food.
I doff clothes, let my skin court
Splashes of jubilation . . .

No land can be, without birds
No globe can be, without hope,
Land begot without labour, being born without lyrics:
The jaunty nationalism
Of the rustics, roof's owners
So fruitfully rustifies.
Population explosion's
A problem. To captive clerks
And the grassland government
Seeing them flooding back is
A nightmare to neat order,
Their land's white-toned unity.
Complexity's in oak-trees,
No land can be, without birds.
What to do with all their joy?
Where to sell woodland concerts?
For cold's sameness – love's bounty:
Birds are a plough to the land.[16]

The statement at the end of the poem is built on a play upon
words which gets lost in translation. *Adar sy'n aradr i'r wlad*,
birds are a plough to the land. There is no resurrection
without the land. There is no civilised land, no ploughed and
cultivated land without the resurrection.

Another variation on this theme, contrasting the mono-
tony of evil and death with the variety of life can be found in
the poems of a sequence written in 1968, after the poet had
almost died of a heart attack brought on by the altitude while
staying in Mexico City. This is one of the most deeply felt of
Bobi Jones' many poetic sequences. In one of its later poems,

as the poet is resting in hospital and already on the way to recovery, he meditates on the banality of death, comparable with the banality of evil.

> But you were no wonder, Death,
> Nor in any way uncommon.
> I saw your stereotyped smile . . .
> You're the One;
> But as for me, I'll go to the diverse, the fullness God
> Created through his imagination,
> The bubbling of passion,
> The various heaps of affection
> Instead of the One grey enemy.

Here we have a picture of divine creativity, not unlike that of Euros Bowen with his creative ferment of divine life and longing. At once Bobi sees this ferment of creativity, this divine fullness, in terms of his friends back home. It is in the variety of our friends, those we love and those who love us, that we see a reflection of the diversity of God.

> I'll celebrate today
> The colours of my friends in Wales,
> One purple in his fidelity,
> Another sun-yellow in generosity,
> And the throng who are white or red-green or lavender
> To their toes in tenderness.
> Since here on my back in hospital
> I can see and hear each one of you
> Make your familiar movements.[17]

Through our friends we participate in resurrection as we recognise again that our life wholly comes from God and can be wholly lived in him.

Bobi Jones is himself a man of great and generous and abundant energy, as we have seen, active in many fields, literary, educational, social, religious. His poetic production is prodigious. Some maintain that he publishes too much. In the 1970s he imposed on himself a time of silence. When he emerged from it in 1986 it was to publish a poem of twenty-one thousand lines '*Hunllef Arthur*, Arthur's Nightmare', the second longest poem in the Welsh language. From the whole, mixed world of that poem, a few quieter lines will remind us how much the writer discovers himself as part of a world which in its very being is created in order to resound the praise of God.

> The hills do not keep silence, for he has purchased
> The creation in the breeze. The maple
> Insists on sharing in the worship; look,
> The ash tree joins with me too. Men are not alone
> Not alien from the creatures; the pebbles
> Of the brook come to chatter their collects
> With me. And when I go wending through the field
> The honey-suckle reaches down its spray
> To shake out God's renown, a fragrance
> Of his praise around me until a scrap of vision
> Of the unseen and unfallen earth and heaven
> Dances through the haze of dawn,
> Promise of the land which was, which shall be.[18]

IV

The great variety of writers whose work we have examined in this book have two things in common. They all sing in praise of God; they all sing in the Welsh language. In these pages we have been concerned with the first of these facts; we must not totally neglect the second. We are living at a time when it is estimated that irreplaceable human languages are dying out as rapidly as irreplaceable species of plants and animals. According to reliable estimates, within the next hundred years the great majority of the languages now spoken on our planet will be extinct. With their death much of what is most distinctively human of us, our capacity to speak and to sing, a capacity necessarily exercised in a particular language, will have died for ever.[19]

This is a frightening thought, and still more frightening because scarcely anyone seems to take account of it. Compared with many of the smaller languages of Asia, Africa or the Americas, languages spoken by a few thousand people, sometimes merely by a few hundred, the future of Welsh may seem assured. Here there are half a million speakers, an abundant literature, not to speak of radio and television. But anyone who knows the situation in Wales or in Ireland or in Brittany, from inside, knows how fragile the position of all these languages is.

Can a language survive, when it no longer has an inner core of monoglot speakers, and when the communities in which it is strong are more and more diluted through the arrival of incomers? We do not know the answer. It may be positive, but statistically and sociologically the future does not look promising. Do the voices we have summoned from the past and the present, speaking of 'the promise of the land which was, the land which shall be', give us grounds for hope? They should at least encourage us not to be mesmerised by figures. Human life is immensely varied, immensely resilient, and always unpredictable. When that frail human life is felt to be sustained by a life beyond this world of space and time, the power of statistics suddenly falters. Meanwhile, at least we can say with Tony Conran,

It is time for the shape of Wales
To have a future.[20]

CHAPTER SEVEN

The Mass on the World:

Saunders Lewis

Themes which we have seen developed in Waldo and Gwenallt, in Euros Bowen and Bobi Jones, are not surprisingly to be found again in different forms in the work of Saunders Lewis. He is the central figure in the mid-twentieth-century renaissance of Christian vision in Welsh writing, and it was perhaps paradoxically his political action which had the greatest impact in the cultural and spiritual sphere. From the burning of the bombing school on the Llŷn Peninsula in September 1936, one of the first public acts of protest against the government in London for four hundred years, much of the subsequent renewal of Welsh life, literary and intellectual perhaps even more than political, has followed directly or indirectly.

To give any full account of Saunders Lewis' Christian vision would be far beyond the scope of these pages. It would need a book of its own. All we shall do here is to look at two quite small poems, though not for that reason insignificant ones, and one very striking prose essay. In them we shall find in miniature many of the fundamental convictions of this writer and something of the ways in which he succeeds in holding together in one, not only apparently contradictory elements in his personal inheritance of faith, but also in the Welsh tradition as a whole. Coming from the family of a

Calvinistic Methodist minister he himself became, by conviction, a firm but never unselfcritical convert to the Catholicism of Rome.

Harri Pritchard Jones, one of the most perceptive commentators on his work, writes about this complex unity of Saunders' faith and vision. It is a faith which can hold together in a single perspective the glory of God's kingdom and the deeply fallen misery of man, which never flinches from looking into the darkness and desolation of our twentieth-century condition. 'In one of his finest poems addressed to The Good Thief, he counterpoints what is seen with the eye of faith – "that a gibbet was the throne of God" – with the view of the faith-less, who saw only "a scarecrow nailed on a pole like a sack of bones" with "flea-ridden robbers as a retinue to his shame". He reveals the total deprivation of the God-man side by side with the glory revealed somehow, for some reason, to this thief. There we see the ex-Calvinist still supremely aware of the gulf between God and man; but there too is the Catholic owing something to Barth, who is so conscious of the humanity of God. Lewis, like Kierkegaard, realised how blind love can be, especially God's, and also how absurd some of our beliefs can look from the proximal side of the chasm between faith and unreason. In himself and in his work he always contained these complexities and paradoxes.'[1] If there is a sense of underlying unity in all this it is one that has been painfully discovered and worked for in the face of much apparent contradiction.

I

One of the underlying themes which has surfaced from time to time throughout this book has been the relationship between the eucharist and the world. God's presence makes the world, we have asserted; but more obviously Christ's presence makes the eucharist. The eucharist then is to be seen not as something set apart in a place of its own. Its place in life and in the world is central. As Saunders Lewis loved to say, 'The Mass makes sense of everything.' Everything is in its own way potentially sacramental and is touched and changed by God's presence in the sacrament.

This sense of a universality of sacramental presence is something which Saunders shared with his great friend David Jones. For David too it was essential to see the mass at the heart of the whole creation. That is what his final and greatest work 'The Anathemata' is all about. Without the mass and what it stands for, the life-giving death of Christ, there is no world at all, merely a random, hostile, ultimately meaningless series of chance events. But without seeing that the mass is rooted in the whole texture of the world, both in its human and in its natural aspects, we shall never be able to understand, let alone rejoice in, the fullness of its purpose and power.

In some ways Saunders Lewis was a typical man of the late twentieth century, painfully conscious of the apparent absence of God from his creation, and of the cruelty and absurdity of our world. But at the same time he was also a man who could be agonisingly aware of God's presence revealed in the beauty of the smallest and most evanescent of things. Here too he stands very close to David Jones and words which he wrote about David's paintings and poems in the catalogue of an exhibition of his work in 1954 could very well be applied to some of his own work: 'The past is all a now, the eternal in the petal, the branches in the clay of a teapot and in the brittleness of glass. The earth herself in her alert pain dreams of the hand that has shaped her. No man nor place stands alone. The scapegoat of Israel is caught in the barbed wire of 1915 and the trees of the field walk in through the windows of your house.' Past and present, the natural world and the human world belong together in one. The whole creation is in the travail of birth. All things point us toward a future which is not yet made known, but which is yet in a mysterious way already present with us. 'David Jones is an artist who affirms that the vision in the final canto of Dante's *Paradiso* is an ever contemporary fact.'[2]

So we may find in Saunders Lewis' work, not only in a major poem like 'Ascension Thursday', which makes constant and deliberate reference to Dafydd ap Gwilym's 'Mass In The Grove', but also a smaller poem like 'The Pine', this sense of the eucharistic quality of all things. In this poem it is not dawn but night. In the quietness of the night a pine tree shoots up toward the heavens like the paschal candle tipped with flame in the darkness of the expectation of the Easter vigil. Slowly the moon rises.

> Hush, the night stands round you in the tranquil chancel
> As heaven's host crosses the earth with its blessing.[3]

The word 'host' here in the original is *afrlladen*, the word for the consecrated eucharistic wafer used by Dafydd ap Gwilym in his springtime poem. The moon is thus a symbol for Saunders of Christ's presence made known in the bread of the altar; benediction indeed.

This sense of the universal significance of the incarnation, and of the incarnation as a light which shines in the world's darkness, is beautifully expressed in a little poem for Christmas which was written in 1958 to be set to music:

> On the ancient tree sprung from Adam's grave,
> Jesse's black and knotted trunk,
> Was grafted a branch from heaven, and today,
> Oh hosanna, Oh hosanna,
> See – here is God's own rose.

The verse points us to the ancient legend that the tree of the cross grew on Adam's grave, indeed that it sprouted from a seed taken from the garden of Eden and placed under Adam's tongue. Out of the dark knotted history of human wrong God is about to make something new. A gift is grafted in which heals and transforms the whole, 'See – here is God's own rose.'

God's gift comes to us in the depths of the night of our separation from him, at the point of despair:

> In the starless night, no moonlight,
> The pit of winter, in the year's
> Senility – behold, a baby,
> The Son of Mary, Oh Sibyl,
> The king of heaven was born.

The world has grown old in its disarray, the human heart has been frozen by the cold of disillusionment. The Roman prophetess speaks of the birth of a child who will renew the circle of the years. This is a birth which brings light and points to a life which shines on the other side of death.

So the whole creation rejoices. The world of nature, the three wise men who come from far lands in the east, the greatest of Latin poets, the incomparable seer of India, all are coming to the birth from beyond the borders of Israel; all share in the rejoicing. For in this birth there is a fulfilment not only of the prophecies of the Old Testament but of the intuitions and aspirations of all peoples and all lands:

> Let a robin sing in the snow,
> Let Melchior sing to his camels,
> Let Virgil sing with the Buddha:
> Son of Mary, Alleluia,
> Eia Jesu, Alleluia,

139

Praise to his name all praise.[4]

The question we are left with is, Is all this a matter of the past? Can it be real for us now?

II

We turn now to an article published in 1955 called 'Students and the Mass'. Forty years ago in the early years of the cold war the possibility of a nuclear holocaust often seemed uncomfortably close. It is true that at one level that danger no longer confronts us. But has our situation really changed at the end of the twentieth century? It does not take much imagination to envisage a situation in a few years' time when the number of powers having nuclear weapons will have increased and the possibility of their use will again have become immediately threatening. Nor are we free from fear of the damage we may do, largely unwittingly, to the global environment, nor from anxiety about the possibilities of violent conflict inherent in the growing inequality between rich nations and poor. On us too, as on our predecessors forty years ago, a sense of the futility of all life can fall, which if it has different motivations has a very similar content.

The question which must have confronted the first Christian generations in Britain after the fall of the Roman Empire still confronts us. If the world is coming to an end very soon, what purpose can there be in carrying on? What reason in particular can be given for carrying on a university life of teaching and research? 'The end of the world, or the end of our world, is near at hand. It's useless to talk about transmitting learning and tradition to the ages to come. There's a good chance that they won't come. The old humanist answers won't do any more nor the modern feckless answer: that man can't help trying to entertain himself as long as he exists and perhaps the odes of the fourteenth century are only a more snobbish form of vanity than filling in Littlewoods football pools.' In face of such a view perhaps the best thing the university teacher can do is put an end to things, 'drive our cars into the waters off the docks'.[5]

There is only one true alternative to this attitude. 'Let us consider another proposition. It is possible that God exists. It is possible for the Christian revelation to be true.' If it is true, then for Saunders everything is different. For if God exists and is present in his world, then everything that exists makes sense, has meaning, whether the world is to end in five minutes' time or in five million years. 'For, according to the Christian revelation, all that is is the creation of God. Therefore the whole history of the universe is in praise of God – *etiam peccata* (even sin) ... And if it is so then for the Christian every science and art is in worship of God. Worship is the raison d'etre of scholarship; because of that the value of scholarship lies beyond accident and is independent of the after effects of any hydrogen bomb.'[6]

The overwhelming sense that the existence of God and the possibility of acknowledging him in this world makes sense of everything was of crucial importance to Saunders Lewis. For him it was simply a matter of life and death. Without it life had no final purpose at all. It was this which drew him to the Roman Church, despite all the problems that move caused for him as a public and political figure in the non-conformist Wales of the thirties. In an interview in 1964 he said, 'I became a Catholic, not because the Catholic social philosophy appealed to me; not at all. I became a Catholic for one terribly simple reason, that I thought that it is through the Catholic Mass that God is worshipped as he ought to be. And that is the only reason that I became a Catholic.'[7]

This sense that the act of worship, and in particular the offering of the sacrifice of the mass, makes present the redeeming reality of God in the midst of our world of time and space, pervades Saunders Lewis' writing and recurs in different forms in different places. But the matter is not so simple as it looks at first. The truth for the sake of which he became a Catholic is something which for him cannot be confined to the Roman Catholic Church.

Thus when we turn back to the article from 1955 we are at once confronted by the fact that for Saunders Lewis the substance of the Catholic faith overflows the borders of the Roman Catholic Church to which he gave his allegiance. The article was published in a small periodical called *Efrydiau Catholig* ('Catholic Studies'); most of its readers would have been students, Welsh-speaking students in the University of Wales. As Saunders Lewis remarks, 'Hardly any of them will be Catholic in name or from conviction. Many may well be Catholic in their hearts and by inclination.' Clearly he is writing for both categories.

Something interesting is happening here. These are the years before Vatican II when the gulf between the Roman Catholic Church and all other Christians was felt to be much deeper than it is today. Saunders is suggesting that there is an underlying substance of Catholic faith, or at least a desire for what is Catholic, present in those who would not use that name, the non-conformists of Wales. He is hinting, as he does in much of his later writing, notably in the short novel about his great-grandparents *Merch Gwern Hywel* (*The Daughter of Gwern Hywel*), that there is a substance of Catholic faith, faith in the Trinity and the incarnation, at the heart of Welsh non-conformity. In particular it is present at the heart of the Methodist tradition in which the previous generations of his family had been nurtured. This creates a unity in despite of all division.

He gave powerful expression to this idea in a lecture on Ann Griffiths, delivered in 1965, and felt at the time, by those who heard it, to be a statement of particular importance to him. At the climax of that lecture he raises again the question whether life can have any ultimate and honourable meaning in a world such as ours, the world of Auschwitz and Buchenwald. He replies by pointing to Ann herself. Ann, he says, responds to this question by everything that she is. 'Ann is a poet putting off her shoes from her feet, because the ground on which she stands at Llanfihangel-yng-Ngwynfa is holy ground. Where there is an object of worship, there cannot be a moment's doubt that life has an eternal meaning and that meaning is everywhere in the universe.'[8]

It is evident that for Saunders Lewis the affirmation which we have been exploring in this book, that God's presence makes the world, needs to become palpable in a very particular way, not just through faith in Christ's incarnation, but through the daily mystery of the mass, the extension of the incarnation, and through the mystery of a life lived in radical conformity with that faith. Then, that particular, lived realisation of God's presence in his world at once leads us to an awareness of his universal presence in the world. The presence is found to be both particular and universal.

Harri Pritchard Jones sums it up admirably when he says of Saunders Lewis, 'He revealed in his work his amazing awareness of the *mysterium tremendum* of "God in the bread" and in his whole universe.'[9] The presence in the sacrament, the presence in the world as sacrament, these things were for him fundamental, inseparable and indispensable.

The fact that for him this presence is to be found throughout creation is thus closely linked to his conviction that the Catholic faith itself can be found beyond the canonical boundaries of the Roman Catholic Church. This was for him much more significant than most of his contemporaries were willing to acknowledge, on whichever side of the Catholic/Protestant divide they stood. Saunders loved to remind his non-conformist colleagues of this substantial shared inheritance of faith, so evident in the original Methodist documents of the eighteenth and nineteenth centuries, in the hymns and sermons as well as in the Confession of Faith of 1823. He was grieved to see 'liberal' theologians who seemed to him to be jettisoning it too easily. So his article on the mass has a kind of ecumenical sub-text about unity which is more important than might at first appear.

At this point we must notice another small but significant feature of the article, which adds to the complexity of the situation but seems to underline this point. It is written as a whole in an easy, colloquial style, but it contains two sentences which are clearly quoted from the Welsh of an earlier age. 'The Great Ruler has placed us at the end of the Ages of Time. . . . The black clawed Destiny which is nigh will snatch away the whole body of Time from us bit by bit.'

Saunders Lewis does not tell us where these words come from, but he does tell us that they were first published in 1701. They are in fact the opening words of the Epistle Dedicatory 'To the Most Reverend Father in Christ, Humphrey Bishop of Bangor', which Ellis Wynne placed at the beginning of his translation of 'Holy Living'. We know of Saunders' regard for Ellis Wynne as a prose stylist but we may well ask ourselves why he chose to quote these two phrases in his essay on the mass. Certainly they are striking enough, but a man of his immense reading could surely have found other dramatic expressions of the sense that time is slipping away from us into eternity. Why did he choose these? Did he have some further purpose? We find on examination that they are the opening words of a letter which soon becomes strongly, indeed violently, polemical against the Church of Rome.

Do we have here simply an expression of Saunders Lewis' mischievous sense of humour? Did he wonder whether

144

anyone would notice where these phrases came from? Or is there something more here, an expression of his sense of the complexity and irony of things? Once we pass beyond the letter of dedication and enter into the substance of Jeremy Taylor's book we find in it one of the fullest and most developed expressions of seventeenth-century Anglican eucharistic doctrine and devotion.

In a previous chapter we have seen a passage of Taylor's about the eucharist as a participation in the eternal offering of Christ, a passage which comes from the first section of the book. In the last chapter of the book, which is dedicated to the subject of preparation for communion, we find another remarkable passage, in the words of an eminent American liturgical scholar, H. Boone Porter, 'Perhaps the most beautiful sentence on this topic ever to be composed in the English language.'

> When the holy man stands at the table of blessing and ministers the rite of consecration, then do as the angels do, who behold and love and wonder, that the Son of God should become food to the souls of his servants; that he who cannot suffer any change or lessening should be broken into pieces and enter into the body to support and nourish the spirit and yet at the same time remain in heaven while he descends to thee upon earth; that he who hath essential felicity should become miserable and die for thee, and then give himself to thee forever to redeem thee from sin and misery; that by his wounds he should procure health to thee, by his affronts he should entitle thee to glory, by his death he should bring thee to life, and by becoming a man he should make thee partaker of the divine nature. These are such glories that although they are made so obvious that each eye may behold them, yet they are also so deep, that no

thought can fathom them: but so it hath pleased him to make these mysteries to be sensible, because the excellency of the depth of the mercy is not intelligible; that while we are ravished and comprehended within the infiniteness of so vast and mysterious a mercy, yet we may be as sure of it, as of that thing we see and feel and smell and taste; but yet is so great that we cannot understand it.[10]

This passage too Ellis Wynne translated with great care, occasionally simplifying the style, sometimes clarifying the meaning. Instead of 'holy man' at the beginning he put simply 'priest', *offeiriad*. Instead of speaking of our redemption from 'misery', he speaks of our redemption from destruction. By the insults Christ sustained we are not only entitled to glory, we are adopted into it and become partakers of the 'nature of God', *natur Dduw*. These are small changes but all work in the same direction, clarifying and emphasising the theological thrust of the passage, the wealth of its sacramental teaching. Taylor's work ends with an extended exhortation to frequent communion, explicitly modelled on a passage from a great Catholic spiritual writer of the early seventeenth century, St Francis de Sales.

All this is interesting enough. Still more interesting is the fact that Taylor, more than most liturgists and theologians of his time, had a strong conviction of the eucharist 'not only as a sacrament of the unity of the Church, but as an instrument of the ultimate unity to which all mankind is called in Christ'. As Boone Porter remarks, 'Taylor has a vision of worship as the glorification of God for all his works in creation, redemption and the glory that is to come, and as involving his blessing on every good aspect of human existence. At the centre of this worship is the "table of blessing", where the promises of the Lord Christ, the head of the Church and first born from the dead, bind heaven and earth together in the representation of the one prevailing sacrifice.' Boone Porter goes on to speak of this vision of liturgical worship as 'an effective sign of peace to the whole human family', a vision which Taylor offers to Christians of every tradition.[11] Here again we see how deeply Taylor was marked by the vision and the spirit of the early Christian centuries.

I am not suggesting that Saunders was necessarily well acquainted with the details of Taylor's sacramental theology. Some of the most important studies of the subject have been published since his time.[12] But he cannot have failed to notice the sacramental emphasis in *Holy Living*; it is indeed strongly brought out by Ellis Wynne himself in his prefatory letter to the reader. All this, I suggest, must have been in his mind in writing this article on the mass, which thus reveals more levels of meaning, a more complex irony, than we might have expected.

What is clear is that both Taylor's work in the seventeenth century and Saunders Lewis' in our own time, have ecumenical implications which have not been fully recognised. They are ecumenical implications which point towards a renewal of integrity and wholeness of vision, an understanding of the Christian faith in its wholeness and balance. This is something which we can find in the early centuries of Christian life in Wales and Ireland, something central to what we now call Celtic Christianity.

Perhaps we had just a glimpse of that ecumenical potential at the time of Saunders Lewis' death in the requiem mass celebrated at his funeral. It was an occasion when the Latin mass drew together a very large gathering of Christians of many denominations, the great majority not Roman Catholic, in a common act of thanksgiving and commemoration. When, after the service in church, some of the congregation moved to the cemetery, the Catholic bishop who had presided over the whole occasion, invited a Presbyterian minister and an Anglican priest to stand beside him at the graveside; it was a small gesture but one not without its symbolism. It revealed again the unexpected capacity of Saunders Lewis' vision to draw people together into new and startling unity.

III

It has, I believe, been important at the end of this book to look at this article in some detail. It recapitulates in a brief space some of the major themes we have been examining earlier. It reveals again the underlying unity of the tradition we have been considering. Still more it suggests that what we now call 'Celtic Christianity' is not a romantic ideal divorced from the complexities of our life in space and time. It is not only a matter of rediscovering early texts from Ireland and Wales, or getting to know the piety of the Western Isles of Scotland in the nineteenth century, however important these things may be.

The Celtic countries, that is to say the countries which have, or have had, Celtic languages and which have sustained cultures deeply marked by a very particular Christian vision, have not ceased to exist during the last four hundred years. Their histories have not been divorced from the history of Western Europe as a whole. It is true that they have experienced that history very differently from the way in which the imperial powers of the West, England, Germany and France, have experienced it.

In the history of Britain and Ireland many events look very different according to where you see them from. People who have suffered history are much closer to their past than peoples who have made history, and they have a different and perhaps deeper insight into it. At this present time prophetic voices of peace make themselves heard from some of the places which have suffered most acutely in the conflicts engendered by the hatreds of Reformation and Counter-Reformation, not least from Belfast itself.

But in and through the vicissitudes of this often tragic history we have tried to suggest, in the later chapters of this book, that vital elements of the earlier vision have survived in powerful and often unnoticed ways. To recover that Celtic vision now, as many seek to do, requires not only an acquaintance with the earliest sources, or a familiarity with the second spring to be found in the theological poetry of mid-twentieth-century Wales, but a willingness to look deeper into the whole mixed period since the Renaissance and the Reformation. It is a period which has within it unexpected possibilities of new life and vision, possibilities which become apparent as we learn to read it in the light of that wholeness which the earliest sources embody so clearly. That is a wholeness which includes grace and nature, creation and redemption, the inward and the outward in such a way that the apparent opposites support and sustain one another. The universal is discovered through the particular, the particular through the universal.

Let R.S. Thomas speak to us of that wholeness of inner and outer, of particular and universal, in lines which come to us from the years spent in the parish of Aberdaron, at the furthest tip of north-west Wales. They are lines which come from the experience of celebrating the eucharist in that church built almost on the sea-shore, open to all weathers, on the frontier between land and sea.

> The breaking of the wave
> outside echoed the breaking
> of the bread in his hands.

149

The crying of sea-gulls
was the cry from the Cross:
Lama Sabachthani. He lifted

the chalice, that crystal in
which love questioning is love
blinded with excess of light.[13]

REFERENCES

Chapter One

1. Charles Thomas. *And Shall These Mute Stones Speak? Post-Roman Inscriptions in Western Britain.* (1994) p.104.
2. *Ibid.* p.322.
3. V. E Nash-Williams. *The Early Christian Monuments of Wales.* (1950) p.84.
4. *Ibid.* p.63.
5. There is a valuable discussion of the relationship between the monastic community and the church as a whole in Philip Sheldrake, *Living Between Worlds: Place and Journey in Celtic Spirituality.* (1995) pp.40–45.
6. A full account of the poem is to be found in Ifor William's *The Beginnings of Welsh Poetry* (1972) pp.100–121. A more recent text and discussion is in Marged Haycock's *Blodeugerdd Barddas O Ganu Crefyddol Cynnar* (1994) pp.3–16. The translation given here is made by Oliver Davies and found in Oliver Davies and Fiona Bowie (eds), *Celtic Christian Spirituality, An Anthology of Medieval and Modern Sources.* (1995) pp.27–8. I am particularly indebted to Paul Quinn in the exegesis of this poem.
7. Jenny Rowland. *Early Welsh Saga Poetry, A Study and Edition of The Englynion,* (1990) pp.289–90.
8. Davies and Bowie. *op. cit.* p.81. From a tenth-century Irish text, 'The Apocalypse of Philip'.
9. For a detailed discussion of Eriugena's position in relation to the Christian East see the articles in Bernard McGinn and Willemien Otten (eds), *Eriugena, East and West* (1994).

151

References

10. John Macquarrie. *In Search of Deity, An Essay in Dialectical Theism.* (1984) p.94 and p.88.
11. The poem is to be found in Marged Haycock, *op. cit.* pp.113–20. Jenny Rowland suggests that these verses are of the same period as the Juvencus *Englynion, op. cit.* pp.289–90. I am indebted to Paul Quinn for the translation of this poem.

Chapter Two

1. Macquarrie. *op. cit.* p.182.
2. Dumitru Staniloae, quoted in A.M. Allchin. *Participation in God.* (1988) pp.71–2.
3. Davies and Bowie *op. cit.* p.28.
4. 'How great and wonderful/it is that the world is not uniform.' Marged Haycock. *op. cit.* p.47.
5. Ecclesiasticus 42:24–5.
6. Tony Conran quoted in *Thirteen Ways of Looking at Tony Conran.* ed. Nigel Jenkins. (1995) pp.32–3.
7. Davies and Bowie. *op. cit.* pp.30–31.
8. Eamonn O'Carrigain. 'The Meeting of St Paul and St Anthony. Visual and Literary Uses of a Eucharistic Motif.' pp.1–58 in G. Mac-Niocall and Patrick Wallace (eds) *Keimeila: Studies in Archaeology and History in Memory of Tom Delaney.* (1988). Nash-Williams thinks it is to be seen on a ninth-century cross slab in South Wales. *op. cit.* pp.157–8.
9. Haycock. *op. cit.* pp.104–113. I am indebted to Paul Quinn for this translation.
10. Davies and Bowie. *op. cit.* p.32.
11. *Ibid.* pp.43–4.
12. *Ibid.* pp.54–6.
13. Tony Conran. *Welsh Verse.* (1986) p.16.
14. R.M. Jones. *Cyfriniaeth Gymraeg.* (1994) pp.114–115.
15. Richard Hooker quoted in C.S. Lewis. *Oxford History of English Literature. The Sixteenth Century, Excluding Drama.* (1954) p.461.

Chapter Three

1. Conran. *op. cit.* p.158.
2. *Ibid.* pp.49–50.
3. R.R. Davies. *The Revolt of Owain Glyn Dŵr.* (1995) p.59.

References

4. Dafydd Johnston. *Iolo Goch: Poems.* (1993) pp.71–3.
5. *Ibid.* pp.114–117.
6. Saunders Lewis. *Meistri'r Canrifoedd.* (1973) pp.80–93. See also R.M. Jones, *Llên Cymru a Chrefydd.* (1977) pp.267–74.
7. I am particularly indebted in this paragraph to my friend Jason Walford Davies.
8. This translation from Davies and Bowie *op. cit.*
9. I have made this version with the help of the two following translations: R.M. Loomis, *Dafydd ap Gwilym. The Poems.* (1981) pp.50–51 and Rachel Bromwich, *Dafydd ap Gwilym. A Selection of Poems.* (1982) pp.196–9.

Chapter Four

1. See Gruffydd Aled Williams. *Ymryson Edmwnd Prys a William Cynwal.* (1986). This magnificent edition of the debate between Prys and Cynwal contains an invaluable introduction surveying Prys' life and work.
2. For a discussion of this poem see A.M. Allchin, *Praise Above All.* (1991) pp.25–9, my translation.
3. Saunders Lewis. *op. cit.* pp.147–52.
4. For Ellis Wynne see Gwyn Thomas, *Ellis Wynne.* (Writers of Wales, 1984).
5. P.G. Stanwood (ed.). *Jeremy Taylor, Holy Living.* (1989) p.35. Ellis Wynne. *Rheol Buchedd Sanctaidd.* (1928 reprint) p.23.
6. *Ibid.* p.39 and p.28.
7. *Ibid.* p.41 and pp.30–31.
8. *Ibid.* p.37 and p.25.
9. See his short novel *The Daughter of Gwern Hywel* in *The Plays of Saunders Lewis, Volume 4.* (Translated Joseph Clancy) pp.25–38. In the same chapter one of the characters remarks 'there's more poetry in the first volume of the "Treasury" than in all the bardic odes of North Wales'.
10. R.M. Jones. *op. cit.* (1977) p.464. See also the chapter on Thomas Jones in the same book, pp.400–411 and R.M. Jones, *Llenyddiaeth Gymraeg, 1936–1972.* (1975) p.241. There is a brief study of Thomas Jones published for the bicentenary of his birth, Frank Price Jones, *Thomas Jones o Ddinbych, 1756–1820.* (1956).
11. *Trysorfa Ysprydol.* (1799) pp.160–61.
12. We are not surprised to find a Wesleyan acquaintance of his com-

153

menting, 'he is possessed of great candour and liberality, and says he knows that God has blessed the preaching of Arminians as well as Calvinists, and that he is perfectly free towards the children of God of every denomination.' Frank Price Jones, *op. cit.* p.18. Unlike most of his co-religionists he also supported Catholic emancipation.

13. *Ibid.* pp.259–60.
14. *Ibid.* pp.220–21.
15. R.S. Thomas. *Collected Poems, 1945–1990.* (1993) pp.470–75.
16. T. Arfon Williams in Daniel Weissbort (ed.) *Modern Poetry in Translation, New Series No.7.* (1995) p.176.
17. Rowan Williams. *After Silent Centuries, Selected Poems.* (1994) p.44.
18. Weissbort. *op. cit.* pp.191–4.

Chapter Five

1. A.M. Allchin and E. de Waal. *Threshold of Light.* (1986) p.39. Translation by H.A. Hodges.
2. Rowan Williams. *op. cit.* p.50.
3. Quoted in A.M. Allchin. *Praise Above All.* (1991) pp.147–8.
4. Seamus Heaney. *The Redress of Poetry.* (1995) p.156.
5. *Ibid.* p.158. On the question of the death-defying quality of art see *Praise Above All*, Chapter 9.
6. Quoted with kind permission from Tony Conran's forthcoming volume of translations of Waldo Williams.
7. *The Dictionary of Welsh Biography Down to 1940.* (1959) p.991. For a discussion of the relationship between journeying and stability in early Christian monasticism see Philip Sheldrake, *Living Between Worlds,* (1995), pp.58–65.
8. As note 6.
9. Ruth Bidgood. *Selected Poems.* (1992) p.85.
10. The original was published in W. Rhys Nicholas, *Beirdd Penfro* (1961) p.158. My translation.
11. R. Gerallt Jones. *Poetry of Wales, 1930–1970.* (1974) pp.112–113.
12. Weissbort. *op. cit.* p.80. Her first English collection, *Parables and Faxes,* was published in 1995.
13. *Ibid.* p.90.
14. *Ibid.* p.32.
15. *Ibid.* pp.84–5.
16. *Ibid.* pp.89–90.

References

Chapter Six

1. *Euros Bowen, Priest-Poet.* Edited Cynthia and Saunders Davies. (1993).
2. Dumitru Staniloae. *The Experience of God, Volume 1.* (1993) p.1.
3. Lars Thunberg. *Microcosm and Mediator.* (second ed. 1995) pp.433–4.
4. C. and S. Davies. *op. cit.* p.133.
5. *Ibid.* pp.57–9.
6. *Ibid.* p.61.
7. *Ibid.* p.117.
8. *Ibid.* p.49.
9. The original of the poem is to be found in Euros Bowen *Detholion*, (1984), pp.60–68. For a discussion of it see A.M. Allchin *The Joy of All Creation*, (second ed. 1993), pp.174–81. I have made use of unpublished notes of the author and of H.A. Hodges who also made an English translation of it.
10. *Eisteddfod Adjudications*, 1963.
11. T.M. Charles-Edwards. *Two Medieval Welsh Poems.* (1971).
12. C. and S. Davies. *op. cit.* p.121.
13. Bobi Jones. *Selected Poems.* Translated by Joseph P. Clancy. (1987) p.12.
14. *Ibid.* pp.31–2.
15. *Ibid.* pp.118–119.
16. *Ibid.* pp.138–9.
17. *Ibid.* p.204.
18. Bobi Jones. *Hunllef Arthur. Cerdd. XII.* ll.330 following. p.114.
19. According to Steven Pinker there are between four thousand and six thousand languages currently spoken on our planet. Of these he estimates as many as 90 per cent will be extinct within the next century. Steven Pinker. *The Language Instinct. The New Science of Language and Mind.* (1994) pp.259–61.
20. Tony Conran. *All Hallows.* (1995).

Chapter Seven

1. Harri Pritchard Jones. *Saunders Lewis: A Presentation of His Work.* (1990) p.8.
2. *Ibid.* p.111.
3. Saunders Lewis. *Selected Poems.* Translated by Joseph P. Clancy. (1993) p.3.
4. *Ibid.* p.40.

References

5. Harri Pritchard Jones. *op. cit.* p.112.
6. *Ibid.* p.113.
7. *Ibid.* p.196.
8. See 'The Place of Ann Griffiths' in Allchin, *Praise Above All*, pp.71–2.
9. Harri Pritchard Jones. *op. cit.* p.16.
10. H. Boone Porter. *Jeremy Taylor: Liturgist.* (1979) p.62. P.G. Stanwood (ed.), *op. cit.*, p.258. Ellis Wynne. *Rheol Buchedd Sanctaidd*, p.253.
11. *Ibid.* pp.160–61.
12. The outstanding work in this connection is H.R. McAdoo, *The Eucharistic Theology of Jeremy Taylor Today* (1988).
13. R.S. Thomas. *The Echoes Return Slow.* (1988) p.69. As in Dafydd ap Gwilym, here too is 'A chalice of ecstasy and love'.

INDEX

Index